50

ASSESSMENT APPROACHES

50

ASSESSMENT APPROACHES

Simple, easy and effective ways to assess learners

SHARRON MANSELL

EDITOR
ANN GRAVELLS

WITH ILLUSTRATIONS BY
ANDREW HAMPEL

Learning Matters
A SAGE Publishing Company
1 Oliver's Yard
55 City Road
London EC1Y 1SP

SAGE Publications Inc.
2455 Teller Road
Thousand Oaks, California 91320

SAGE Publications India Pvt Ltd
B 1/I 1 Mohan Cooperative Industrial Area
Mathura Road
New Delhi 110 044

SAGE Publications Asia-Pacific Pte Ltd
3 Church Street
#10-04 Samsung Hub
Singapore 049483

Editor: Amy Thornton
Senior project editor: Chris Marke
Project management: Deer Park Productions
Marketing manager: Lorna Patkai
Cover design: Wendy Scott
Typeset by: C&M Digitals (P) Ltd, Chennai, India
Printed in the UK

Library of Congress Control Number: 2020930957

British Library Cataloguing in Publication Data

A catalogue record for this book is available from the British Library

ISBN 978-1-5264-9318-7
ISBN 978-1-5264-9317-0 (pbk)

At SAGE we take sustainability seriously. Most of our products are printed in the UK using responsibly sourced papers and boards. When we print overseas we ensure sustainable papers are used as measured by the PREPS grading system. We undertake an annual audit to monitor our sustainability.

Contents

Acknowledgements

I would like to give a special thanks to the following people who have helped me with the production of this book. They have freely given their time, knowledge and advice, which has resulted in some excellent contributions and additions to the content. Without their amazing proofreading skills and honest feedback, this book would not be what it is, and I am truly grateful.

Adrienne Pye – External Quality Assurer at VTCT

Gill Burdett – Assistant Principal, White Rose Beauty Colleges Derby (Retired)

Lisa Morris – BA (Hons), PGCE, FCIEA, Director at Educating UK & Lead External Quality Assurer at TQUK

Louise C Gulbrandsen – QTS Med, Teacher at Loavenstad School

Rick Mills – Technical Training Specialist at United Utilities Water Ltd

I would like to express a special thank you to my boss, Karen Lee-Cooke, Principal of the White Rose Beauty Colleges, for her words of encouragement and the trust and opportunities she has given me.

I would like to thank Richard, Emma, Steven and Morgan for their continued support and patience.

I would also like to thank my Senior Commissioning Editor (Education) Amy Thornton for her support and guidance.

This book would not have happened without the help and support from my editor Ann Gravells and my illustrator Andrew Hampel. So a huge thanks to them.

Every effort has been made to trace the copyright holders and to obtain their permission for the use of copyright material. The publisher, editor and author will gladly receive any information enabling them to rectify any error or omission in subsequent editions.

Sharron Mansell

Author statement

Sharron Mansell

Sharron started delivering education and training programmes on a part-time basis in 1987, before progressing into a full-time career in further education in 2000. She has gained practical work-based skills and a wide and varied understanding of schools' provision, further and higher education, apprenticeships and full-cost courses.

Starting her career as a teacher in a land-based specialist college, she progressed to course management before taking responsibility for several departments within a large further education college. Sharron further developed her knowledge and skills within the sector when her role changed to Head of Services to Business. She is the Assistant Principal of Quality at the White Rose Beauty Colleges and their Ofsted nominee. It is recognised as the UKs largest beauty therapy training provider which was judged Outstanding by Ofsted in 2019.

Sharron is passionate about raising standards in education and is committed to supporting quality improvement at all levels and stages. As well as her work in further education she has also worked with primary and secondary schools as a governor to support quality improvement.

Sharron holds an Honour's Degree in Education and Training, has a Certificate in Education, is a Member of the Society for Education and Training, and holds QTLS status.

She is the author of:

50 Teaching and Learning Approaches

Achieving QTLS Status

Sharron can be contacted via:

Facebook: https://www.facebook.com/mansellsharron/

Twitter: https://twitter.com/sharronmansell

LinkedIn: https://www.linkedin.com/in/sharronmansell

Email: sharronmansell@outlook.com

Editor statement

Ann Gravells

Ann has been teaching, assessing and quality assuring in the further education and training sector since 1983. She is a director of her own company *Ann Gravells Ltd*, an educational consultancy based in East Yorkshire. She specialises in teaching, training, assessment and quality assurance.

Ann holds a Master's in Educational Management, a PGCE, a Degree in Education, and a City & Guilds Medal of Excellence for teaching. She is a Fellow of the Society for Education and Training, and holds QTLS status.

Ann has been writing and editing text books since 2006, which are mainly based on her own experiences as a teacher and the subsequent education of trainee teachers. She aims to write in plain English to help anyone with their role. She creates resources for teachers and learners such as PowerPoints, online courses and handouts for the assessment, quality assurance, and teacher training qualifications. These are available via her website: www.anngravells.com

Ann has worked for several awarding organisations producing qualification guidance, policies and procedures, and carrying out the external quality assurance of teaching, assessment and quality assurance qualifications.

She is an Ofqual Assessment Specialist, a consultant to The University of Cambridge's Institute of Continuing Education, and a technical advisor to the awarding organisation Training Qualifications UK (TQUK).

Illustrator statement

Andrew Hampel

Andrew is a designer and lecturer who has been delivering and managing further and higher education art and design courses for 20 years. His design work ranges from traditional watercolour to multimedia video performance pieces.

Outside education, Andrew is a partner in an event company *District 14*, providing marketing and corporate presentations for comic cons.

Having a direct link to the vocational design industry gives his students an excellent opportunity to work directly with his company to provide workshops and materials to the community, along with access to a wide range of professionals including Marvel and BBC Books.

As well as design work, Andrew has a passion for history and is a trustee for a World War Two home front project. He has a special responsibility for educational projects and community outreach.

Andrew has contributed writing to a number of science fiction anthology works and podcasts as well as writing and illustrating *Quick Histories of Hull*.

Andrew's Online Folio can be seen at – deviantart.com/skaromedia

Andrew can be contacted via email – skaromedia@hotmail.com

Foreword

If you are looking for innovative, yet easy and effective ways to assess your learners, then the chapters in this book are just what you need.

Whether you are new to assessment or are an experienced assessor, these approaches will give you lots of ideas to put theory into practice. They might help you to try something different or to adapt what you currently do.

Just like Sharron's book *50 Teaching and Learning Approaches*, I wished a book like this had been available when I first started assessing learners. It's fine to read text books all about the theory of assessment, but it's putting it into practice that matters, to confirm a learner's progress and achievements.

Sharron has included a few traditional assessment approaches such *assignments, observation* and *questioning*, and added lots of other exciting approaches such as *digital storytelling, exit and entry tickets, photographic testimony* and *two-stage digest.*

Do try out some or all of the approaches, and feel free to adjust them to suit your subject, your learners, and the environment within which learning is taking place. However, if you are summatively assessing towards a qualification, standard or programme, you may need to check the requirements of the relevant organisation or body.

You will find Appendix 1 will prove useful if you are involved in the training or assessment of apprentices. Appendix 2 will explain the difference between marking and grading, and Appendix 3 outlines how to make a decision and provide feedback to learners. Appendix 4 touches on quality assurance, an important aspect of the assessment process.

Both Sharron and I hope you enjoy the book. Please feel free to give us some feedback here: http://www.anngravells.com/anns-books/book-reviews

Other books in the series:

50 Teaching and Learning Approaches

50 Quality Assurance Approaches (coming soon)

Ann Gravells
www.anngravells.com

Introduction

Your role

Your role as an assessor can have a big impact on the lives of the learners being assessed. It is therefore important that the assessment process is carried out with integrity, and is as supportive and non-threatening as possible. Carried out well, the assessment process can positively influence an individual's life and future employment prospects. This is whether they are going into their first job; reskilling to have a change in their career; upskilling to go for a promotion; or to take up self-employment.

Assessment should never be overused to cause unnecessary work for the learner. It should ensure learning has taken place, and that learners have committed their new skills, behaviours, attitudes, knowledge and understanding to their long-term memory.

You should carefully plan activities which support learners to fully engage in the assessment process, and that have a positive impact on their progression. This book will support you to do just that.

Using this book

This book is not about theory, it's about giving you some ideas of assessment activities to try out. It is aimed at assessing learners of all ages from primary school through to university. It has many examples of formative assessments which you can use for apprentices prior to end-point summative assessment (which can then only be undertaken by end-point assessors).

Throughout the book you will find traditional approaches that have been recognised as good practice for years as well as many new activities. They might not all work, perhaps due to different group dynamics, or the maturity of your learners, or you might decide to adapt them to suit your own learners' requirements. Many of the activities can be used informally to prepare learners for formal assessment.

The chapters are set out in alphabetical order and you may choose to read the book from start to finish, or to select a title from the contents page and locate a specific assessment approach.

At the end of the chapters you will find useful appendices regarding: apprenticeship programmes; marking and grading; making assessment decisions and providing feedback to learners, and quality assurance.

The word *learner* has been used throughout the book to describe the person being assessed, which includes apprentices. The word *assessor* has been used to describe the person carrying out the assessment activity which includes teachers, trainers, tutors, coaches, facilitators and lecturers.

Chapter grids

Each chapter starts with a grid to indicate whether the activity is suitable for an *individual* learner, a *small group* or a *large group*. It indicates if the approach is suitable for *initial, formative, summative, informal or formal* assessment. It includes a tick box to indicate if there is any *preparation and marking* required. It also specifies the academic *level* the approach could suit.

Chapter structure

Each chapter has a series of headings to help you understand how to use the activities.

What is it and where can it be used? – an explanation of what the activity is, how to set it up and where is can be used.

What can it be used for? – suggests how best you can use the activity to carry out assessment.

Resources – lists materials and equipment that might be required to undertake the activity.

Advantages – lists the benefits of using the activity.

Disadvantages – lists difficulties or challenges you may find with the activity.

Some of the chapters have specific examples, and at the end of every chapter you will find a handy *tip* and a short list of references for *further reading and weblinks*.

The chapters are illustrated with characters who are non-gender specific and reflect inclusivity, equality and diversity.

Types of assessment

Initial assessment is the process of establishing a learner's starting point, and identifying any additional needs that a learner might have. This enables you to plan a learning programme which is structured and relevant to them. The information also supports you to plan the sequence of the curriculum to enable learners to build upon previous learning, and to develop the new knowledge and skills they need. Planning and record keeping is an important part of the assessment process, not only at the start, but also throughout each learner's journey. Standardisation of practice between assessors of the same subject will ensure a fair service is given to learners.

Formative assessment includes ongoing activities which can be used formally or informally. These are to monitor or measure a learner's progress towards a qualification or learning target. It can take place at any point in the learner's journey and in any environment and context. Its interpretations and actions should be carefully planned and informed by you and your organisation's intent, e.g. why do you need to carry out the assessment, how often do you need to measure a learner's progress, how much time will it take to carry out the assessment activities, how will you collate the results and analyse your findings? In addition, how will you use and act upon your findings to inform improvement?

Formative assessment should always enable learners to demonstrate what they know and can do, and what else they need to be able to do to be successful in their learning. The results from any formative assessment should inform the next stage of planning in regard to teaching and learning, e.g. are they ready for summative assessment or do they need further training?

Examples of formative assessment include: cards and games; peer assessment; quizzes; and role play.

Summative assessment is used at the end of a qualification, unit, module or learning target to evaluate the learning which has taken place towards the required outcomes. The marking and grading criteria are usually set by an awarding organisation, and they detail the evidence requirements which must be met to achieve a pass. Some awarding organisations include a scoring matrix to distinguish between a pass and a better pass, such as *pass*, *merit* or *distinction*, which are commonly used in accredited qualifications. Further information regarding marking and grading can be found in Appendix 2.

Examples of summative assessment include: end-point assessment; a final project; assignment; portfolio; or an examination.

Informal assessment is an approach used to measure a learner's progress which can easily be embedded into a session. It is based on the content of the session and how well the learners are progressing at that time. It does not measure academic achievement or allow comparisons to other learners, national averages or benchmarks. An informal assessment approach could be an assessor asking a learner questions to gain responses to help measure that learner's progress to date. Informal assessment approaches are usually formative.

Formal assessment is an approach used to measure a learner's achievement; it measures what and how well a learner has learned something. The results can be used to measure one learner against another or to compare results against national averages or benchmarks. A formal assessment approach could be the awarding organisation setting and marking an exam such as a GCSE. Formal assessment approaches are usually summative.

Whichever assessment approach you use, you will need to interpret and record the results and assessment data in line with the awarding organisation's and/or your organisation's policies and procedures.

Education Inspection Framework

In September 2019, Ofsted introduced the Education Inspection Framework (EIF) which replaced the Common Inspection Framework (CIF). The EIF focuses on what is being taught and how it is being assessed, rather than being based on results and outcomes.

The new framework includes the *quality of education* based on curriculum and outcomes, the *behaviour and attitudes* of learners, the *personal development* of learners and *leadership and management*. Under the quality of education, three key aspects are measured: these are *intent, implementation* and *impact,* known as the three *Is* in regard to curriculum and the sequencing of the curriculum. Introducing the proposed changes in October 2018 Amanda Spielman stated:

> Under quality of education, we intend to look at 3 distinct aspects. First the intent – what is it that schools want for all their children? Then the implementation – how is teaching and assessment fulfilling the intent? Finally, the impact – that is the results and wider outcomes that children achieve and the destinations that they go on to.

The 3 Is can be interpreted in a similar way for assessment, for example:

- *Intent* – Why are you carrying out the assessment? Is it necessary? Who is the assessment for and what do you expect to achieve?
- *Implementation* – How will you carry out the assessment, is the assessment approach fair and inclusive, and how will you ensure the learner understands the process?
- *Impact* – What difference will it make to the learner once you have completed the assessment?

Throughout the assessment activities, you should always demonstrate integrity and professionalism to your learners to enable them to learn from you and model your behaviour. In addition, always check the spelling, grammar and punctuation of anything you show or hand out to your learners to support them to improve their own skills.

Further reading and weblinks

Gov.UK – *Amanda Spielman's speech to the SCHOOLS NorthEast Summit* – https://tinyurl.com/y5d7xwh7

Gov.UK – *Further education and skills inspection handbook* – https://tinyurl.com/y6es6aun

Gravells A (2016) *Principles and Practices of Assessment*: Learning Matters/SAGE, London.

Mansell S (2019) *50 Teaching and Learning Approaches*: Learning Matters/SAGE, London.

1 Assignments

Individual	√	Small group	√	Large group	√
Initial	*	Formative	√	Summative	√
Informal	√	Formal	√	Preparation and marking	√
Entry Level	√	Level 1 and 2	√	Level 3 upwards	√

depends upon what and how you are planning to use the approach

What is it and where can it be used?

An assignment is about setting a relevant piece of work based on a particular topic or subject for the learner to carry out. It should encourage some independent reading or research, and can be written, verbal or practical. The assignment can be set as a homework task, but you would need to allow yourself time in a session to introduce it. Alternatively, it can be set as a task to complete during the session. Additionally, assignments can be used as a group activity to develop skills such as collaboration and communication. You can give additional tasks to those learners who have not clearly demonstrated the required criteria.

Competence, skills, behaviours, attitudes, knowledge and/or understanding is measured by assessing the completed assignment. The feedback you give should be developmental and constructive, not just descriptive (see Appendix 3).

Assignments can be internally set and marked, i.e. by yourself, or externally set and marked, i.e. by an awarding organisation. If they are being used as a formal summative assessment activity, they must be produced in a way which measures the required criteria, be completed individually by each learner within a set time frame, and follow all awarding organisation requirements for assessment and feedback.

What can it be used for?

An assignment can be practical or theoretical, carried out during a session or outside of the session, depending on how you wish to use it. For example, to ascertain an individual's knowledge prior to starting a topic or subject you could ask them to complete a written assignment which would enable you to tailor your delivery at the correct level. This would be classed as *initial* assessment. To measure a learner's progress towards a practical task you could give them an assignment brief asking them to complete it outside of the session (perhaps as part of a work placement) and then complete a reflective log (see Chapter 32). This could be classed as *formative* or *summative* assessment.

Although an assignment is primarily used to assess competence, skills, behaviours, attitudes, knowledge and/or understanding, it can also be used as a teaching approach to enable learning to take place through collaborative working, further reading and research.

Setting differentiated assignments (i.e. at different levels), or setting work with the option to complete a further higher-level task, will enable stretch and challenge. For example, the assignment could be to draw, name and label the muscles and tendons in a human being's leg. The optional task could be to describe the function of one of the named muscles and one of the named tendons.

If you are using assignments for summative assessment, you will need to ensure the work is the learner's own by asking them to sign an authenticity declaration, or by using exam conditions with an invigilator present.

Resources

- ICT equipment with word-processing facilities for creating a written assignment or pens and paper
- Printer/copier (if the written assignment is not accessible electronically by the learners)
- Relevant items, and equipment for the topic or subject

Advantages

- Supports identifying individuals who are struggling with a concept or subject
- Encourages independent thinking and research skills
- Can be created, completed and accessed electronically
- Can challenge a learner's potential
- Can be used formatively or summatively

Disadvantages

- Can be time-consuming to plan, assess, and to provide individual feedback
- Can cause some learners to feel anxious and overwhelmed
- If set as a homework task, it can be difficult to know if it is the learner's own work (an authenticity declaration could be signed by the learner)
- If you are using a written assignment for learners with special educational needs and disabilities (SEND), they may require more processing time to read through the text and comprehend meaning

Tip

You should communicate how and when the mark and/or feedback will be given. You can manage learner expectations by explaining the marking and quality assurance processes.

Further reading and weblinks

Bates B (2016) *A Quick Guide to Special Needs and Disabilities*: SAGE, London

Gravells A (2016) *Principles and Practices of Assessment*: Learning Matters/SAGE, London.

Mansell S (2019) *50 Teaching and Learning Approaches*: Learning Matters/SAGE, London.

Tips on writing assignments – https://tinyurl.com/jkqh3p7

2 Cards and games

Individual	√	Small group	√	Large group	√
Initial	*	Formative	√	Summative	
Informal	√	Formal		Preparation and marking	√
Entry Level	√	Level 1 and 2	√	Level 3 upwards	*

*depends upon what and how you are planning to use the approach

What is it and where can it be used?

Cards and games are fun ways to assess if learning has taken place, e.g. to match, list, order or group items relating to the current topic or subject. Below are five examples of quick and simple assessment approaches using cards and games. If you don't have any card, you could write on strips of firm paper.

1. List about ten questions and answers (on separate pieces of card) relating to the current topic. Learners can match the answers to the questions. A discussion can take place if any were matched wrongly.

2. List a few topic headings and related points (e.g. recipes [headings] and ingredients [points]) on separate pieces of card. Learners can list the points under each heading. A discussion can take place as to what is correct or not.

3. List a few actions (on separate pieces of card) which need to be carried out in a certain order, e.g. the procedures which must be carried out for a certain process to occur. Learners can then place these in the order which they think is correct. A discussion can take place as to what is correct or not.

4. List a few headings with related items which learners need to group together (on separate pieces of card), e.g. different aspects of a particular job and the tools required for each. Learners need to group the tools according to the jobs. A discussion can take place as to what is correct or not.

5. Create related topic cards in pairs, e.g. for a group studying English, the cards could be words which are synonyms or antonyms. Or for a group studying maths, one card could have a sum and the other card has the correct answer. Or for vocational subjects, a group studying sports may have a card with the word or image of goal posts and the matching card is the word or image of a goalkeeper. Learners are handed one card each and need to move around the learning environment to find another learner and match two related cards.

What can it be used for?

Cards and games' tasks can be used for informal formative assessment to check progress, knowledge and understanding of related themes. It enables learners to demonstrate that they can recall and have remembered information over a period of time.

You should observe the task and listen to the learners' discussions; any misconceptions should be corrected immediately. Informal feedback should be provided to the learners at the end of the task, identifying areas for improvement or development.

Resources

- The cards or game

Advantages

👍 Learner centred

👍 Supports memory recall to check if learners can remember information over a period time

👍 Great for learners who are usually unwilling to participate in group assessment activities

Disadvantages

👎 Time-consuming to create and set up (but can be used for future groups)

👎 Can cause too much competitiveness (if used as a group or paired activity)

👎 Can seem trivial to some learners

> **Tip**
>
> If you laminate the cards, they can be used again for future groups.

Further reading and weblinks

Kirstens Kaboodle – *Top ten task card activities* – https://tinyurl.com/yb662nvz

Icebreakers.ws – *Who's my match?* – https://tinyurl.com/y3ffb3v3

Mansell S (2019) *50 Teaching and Learning Approaches*: Learning Matters/SAGE, London.

3   Case study

Individual	√	Small group	√	Large group	*
Initial		Formative	√	Summative	√
Informal	√	Formal	√	Preparation and marking	√
Entry Level		Level 1 and 2	√	Level 3 upwards	√

*depends upon what and how you are planning to use the approach

What is it and where can it be used?

A case study is a description of a real-life situation which enables a learner to explore an in-depth scenario and demonstrate what they would do. It can be hypothetical or real, complete or incomplete depending on the required outcome. It is suitable for small groups of learners or for individuals. A single case study can be used which requires different solutions, or different case studies can be given to each group or individual. It can be paper based or electronic, e.g. using a range of media.

It enables learners to demonstrate their competence, skills, behaviours, attitudes, knowledge and/or understanding. If used as a group activity, team-working skills such as collaboration and effective communication could also be assessed. It can be used as a teaching approach to enable learning to take place through further reading and research.

Clear assessment criteria are critical to the success of this assessment approach. Consideration regarding dividing the case study into sections with marks for each will support learners to clarify the requirements. You will need to check the assessment criteria and requirements from the awarding organisation if you are using this approach as summative assessment for an accredited qualification.

What can it be used for?

The case study can be formative or summative and can be used in three different ways to assess learners:

1. As part of their course work, a group of four to six learners are presented with a complex situation and must solve a problem. They should discuss the problem and consider all possible solutions, finally agreeing which is the best scenario or solution. Learners can be given all the relevant material relating to the case study; or to stretch and challenge, research activities could be set in relation to problem solving.

2. A time-constrained exam where the individual learner reads the case study and then answers related questions under exam conditions.

3. Individually, learners present their own case study demonstrating their knowledge and skills from their own experiences, e.g. a learner undertaking a Level 4 Business Management programme needs to write a business plan. Using the case-study method, they are able to demonstrate a wide selection of information and data analysis used to support their decision making regarding the location of suitable premises for their business.

Resources

- Depends upon what and how you are planning to use the approach

Advantages

- Supports the development of research and reflective skills
- Encourages independent thinking
- Develops problem-solving skills
- Can be motivational
- Builds on current knowledge, skills and understanding

Disadvantages

- Can be time-consuming to set up, assess and provide feedback
- Must have clear outcomes
- Difficult to know the individual input if learners are working in groups

---

Tip

Learners could undertake class-based presentations of their case study to their peers, to gain feedback from them.

Further reading and weblinks

Mansell S (2019) *50 Teaching and Learning Approaches*: Learning Matters/SAGE, London.

The Higher Education Academy – *Teaching materials using case studies* – https://tinyurl.com/cc88qjh

The London School of Economics and Political Science – *Case studies* – https://tinyurl.com/y65fmjh5

4   Charts and posters

Individual	√	Small group	√	Large group	*
Initial		Formative	√	Summative	√
Informal	√	Formal	√	Preparation and marking	√
Entry Level	√	Level 1 and 2	√	Level 3 upwards	√

*depends upon what and how you are planning to use the approach

What is it and where can it be used?

Charts and posters are an alternative to traditional assessment approaches such as exams, case studies and essays. They are a visual display of the content and findings of a topic or subject, and can be created electronically or by hand, e.g. an academic poster could summarise information from a research topic, whereas a vocational poster could summarise key information in relation to health and safety. The structure of the chart or poster should have a clear beginning, middle and end, and should group related information together; it is also useful to give a maximum word count. The assessment approach for charts and posters measures the content, structure and presentation of information provided by the learner.

What can it be used for?

Charts and posters can be used informally or formally as an individual or group assessment approach. They are learner centred, and using them as a group approach develops learners' communication and team-building skills, as well as encouraging independence. Charts and posters are a brilliant approach for formative assessment. They allow learners to explore a topic or subject and receive constructive feedback to further develop their knowledge, understanding and skills. Through the creation of a chart or poster, learners can demonstrate their knowledge and understanding using creative skills. This can be further developed by the learners presenting their chart or poster to an audience, e.g. learners can create a chart or poster, display it and present their creation back to their peers. Peer assessment (see Chapter 21) can also be used to provide formative assessment.

Charts and posters can also be used for summative assessment. These are becoming increasingly popular in higher education as an assessment approach that encourages the learners to take control of their learning to become self-directed.

Resources

- Computer software and a printer if creating electronically
- Large paper and a range of coloured pens or paints (if creating by hand)

Advantages

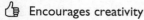 Encourages creativity

Develops problem-solving and critical-thinking skills

Develops independence and confidence

Develops collaboration and team-building skills (if used as a group approach)

Disadvantages

Learners could focus on the creative aspect rather than the content

Can be difficult for a learner to correct if a mistake is made

Assessment can be subjective

Not all learners will engage with a practical activity

Tip

Explain to your learners that the content of the chart or poster should *tell a story* and focus on a few key points. This will help them to produce a concise piece of work.

Further reading and weblinks

Assessment Resources – *Types of Assessment Methods: Poster* – https://tinyurl.com/y564atfx

The London School of Economics and Political Science – *Posters* – https://tinyurl.com/y5md8b55

5   Checklist

Individual	√	Small group	√	Large group	√
Initial	*	Formative	√	Summative	*
Informal	√	Formal	*	Preparation and marking	√
Entry Level	*	Level 1 and 2	*	Level 3 upwards	√

*depends upon what and how you are planning to use the approach

What is it and where can it be used?

A checklist is a paper or electronic document which can be used to identify the presence or absence of a learner's competence, skills, behaviours, attitudes, knowledge and/or understanding. It can be used for written or practical assessment activities. The checklist should have clear criteria based on the required outcomes. It could have tasks put together into sections, or run in an order from start to finish.

Itemised tasks should be listed at one side of the checklist and a space provided at the other side for learners to add evaluative or reflective comments as they complete each section or task. The tasks should be concise, no more than two pages of A4 paper, and must be worded carefully to avoid any misinterpretation by the learners.

Alternatively, a checklist could be used by an assessor to *tick off* aspects which a learner has completed. The assessor can add specific comments for each aspect, e.g. when observing a practical activity.

What can it be used for?

A checklist is a great way to formatively assess learner progress towards a summative outcome, e.g. learners undertaking a first-aid course must follow a sequenced routine when first arriving at the scene of an accident. Learners could complete a checklist as they watch a video of a simulated accident scene with first aiders tending to the casualties. Learners will evaluate their progress towards the tasks on the checklist, stating what was good practice and what was poor practice. They should also evaluate if anything was missed, or if it could have been done in a different way.

The benefit of writing the tasks in a sequence order supports learners to focus on the key areas you wish them to develop, and by completing an evaluation of what they see, enables you to formatively assess their progress. The individual responses will enable you to ascertain where each learner is regarding their knowledge and understanding. This will support you to identify which of your learners are ready for summative assessment and which learners require further development.

Resources

- A checklist relating to the topic or subject
- Pens and paper or a suitable electronic device

Advantages

👍 Supports identifying individuals who are struggling with a concept

👍 Can be adapted to use as paired work or small group work

👍 Develops reflective thinking skills

👍 Promotes spontaneous writing skills and self-confidence

Disadvantages

👎 Time-consuming to produce (but can be used for future learners)

👎 Individual support and supervision might be required

👎 Can cause some learners to feel anxious and under pressure

Tip

This activity can be adapted to use on learning platforms such as a virtual learning environment (VLE), as an extension activity or as homework.

Further reading and weblinks

LD@school – *Checklists and achievement charts* – https://tinyurl.com/y2kr4ukz

Teachthought – *How a simple checklist can improve learning* – https://tinyurl.com/y4gcnb6h

6 Digital storytelling

Individual	√	Small group	√	Large group	√
Initial	*	Formative	√	Summative	√
Informal	√	Formal	√	Preparation and marking	√
Entry Level	*	Level 1 and 2	√	Level 3 upwards	√

depends upon what and how you are planning to use the approach

What is it and where can it be used?

Digital storytelling is about learners using computer-based technology to create evidence which can be assessed formally towards a qualification, or informally to measure a learner's progress towards a particular subject. For example, learners are given a topic to research and must use computer-based technology to create a story about the research they have undertaken. This could be a documentary regarding their experience of accessing the research, what they found out and a summary of their findings. Learners can use a camera on a mobile phone or a similar device to capture short videos and photographs, or use copyright-free images from the internet to tell their story.

Digital storytelling can be used in the classroom or set as a homework task. The final edited story should be between five and ten minutes in total time. Learners should include *selfies*, e.g. a *selfie* of them accessing materials in a public library or a *selfie* of them carrying out research using a computer. The *selfie* images will support authenticating the learner's story.

Prior to starting this approach, learners must be educated about plagiarism and unfair means of access. Alternatively, learners could be requested to only use their own images.

What can it be used for?

Digital storytelling can be used as an alternative to written assignments, presentations, case studies, projects, a demonstration, or problem sets. If you are using digital storytelling for summative assessment for an accredited qualification, you would need to check with the awarding organisation that it is acceptable, before submitting it as evidence.

Digital storytelling is also a fun formative assessment approach which allows learners to be as creative as they like. For example, a non-accredited Equine Clipping course might require learners to recognise a range of clips and to undertake four of them. Learners could combine photographs, short videos and text to make a story of the clips they have practised and use stock images to show the clips they have not yet attempted. They could use *selfies* mimicking emojis to demonstrate their reactions towards attempting the different styles of clips. The digital story can be shared with a peer to gain their feedback.

It is a good activity for an individual or group assessment approach. However, if you are using it as a group approach, learners must identify and agree roles and responsibilities to ensure all group members are involved. You would also need to assess who has contributed to what when making a decision.

Resources

- A digital camera (e.g. a mobile phone with a built-in camera)
- Access to the internet
- Relevant computer software or apps
- Digital device or cloud-based storage to save the work

Advantages

- 👍 Develops computer skills
- 👍 Can be fun
- 👍 Encourages creativity
- 👍 Develops problem-solving and critical-thinking skills
- 👍 Develops collaboration and team-building skills (if used as a group approach)

Disadvantages

- 👎 Learners need access to relevant devices and a mobile camera
- 👎 Learners could focus on the creative aspect rather than the content
- 👎 Assessment can be subjective
- 👎 Not all learners will take it seriously

Tip

There are many free digital storytelling tools available via the internet which learners can access and download to help them construct and create their digital story. Just carry out a search to see what you can find.

Further reading and weblinks

Educational uses of Digital Storytelling – *What is digital storytelling?* – https://tinyurl.com/yyzbtxdt

The London School of Economics and Political Science – *Visual media* – https://tinyurl.com/y2cfef56

White J (2015) *Digital Literacy Skills for FE Teachers*: Learning Matters/SAGE, London.

7 Discussions and debates

Individual		Small group	√	Large group	
Initial	*	Formative	√	Summative	√
Informal	√	Formal	√	Preparation and marking	
Entry Level	√	Level 1 and 2	√	Level 3 upwards	√

*depends upon what and how you are planning to use the approach

What is it and where can it be used?

A discussion or a debate involves two or more learners talking about a specific topic or subject to reach a decision, or to exchange ideas and views. It could be used to deliberate and contemplate a topic or subject with opposing sides, or as a fact-finding conversation. It can be formal or informal, individual or group based depending on the required outcome.

Assessment is undertaken by means of observed and auditory evidence, with judgements being made towards set criteria.

What can it be used for?

Discussions or debates are a great assessment approach which can improve learners' communication skills in preparation for employment. They can be used to measure learners' preparation, organisational and presentation skills as well as their use of technical language.

Discussions or debates can be used formatively to support the improvement of learners' speaking and listening skills, or as a summative approach. For example, learners undertaking a Level 1 Functional Skills qualification are required to *take part in a formal and informal discussion and exchanges that include unfamiliar subjects*. Formative assessment of the discussion could take place with the learners by giving them relevant tasks to practise, and to receive feedback regarding their performance. Formative assessment could also include electronic visual recording of the learners undertaking a discussion, and allowing them to view their own performance to enable them to improve further. Once learners are fully prepared, summative assessment can take place under formal supervision. This could either be by the assessor observing the discussion live or by viewing an electronic visual recording of the learners.

For the purpose of functional skills, learners are assessed regarding their performance on an individual basis towards the requirements of the awarding organisation's descriptors. However, if you are using this approach as an informal assessment method, criteria could be developed to measure group performance.

Resources

- A list of questions, topic or subject to base the discussion or debate on

Advantages

👍 Learner centred

👍 Helps to develop speaking and listening skills

👍 Supports the development of analytical and critical thinking skills

👍 Helps increase learner confidence and self-esteem in preparation for employment

Disadvantages

👎 Can be time-consuming

👎 Can be difficult to keep learners on task

👎 Not all learners will engage in this approach, particularly if they are shy or less confident

👎 Some learners might dominate, or become loud if the groups are not managed effectively throughout the activity

---

Tip

Make sure learners understand the context of the discussion or debate, and how long they have to carry it out.

Further reading and weblinks

Educationworld – *Debates in the classroom* – https://tinyurl.com/y36m2t7c

Mansell S (2019) *50 Teaching and Learning Approaches*: Learning Matters/SAGE, London.

TeachHub – *How to hold a classroom debate* – https://tinyurl.com/y2yu8rnm

Teachingonpurpose – *Discussion in the classroom: Why do it, how to do it, and how to assess it* – https://tinyurl.com/yyxtreyt

8   End-point assessment

Individual	√	Small group		Large group	
Initial		Formative		Summative	√
Informal		Formal	√	Preparation and marking	√
Entry Level		Level 1 and 2	√	Level 3 upwards	√

What is it and where can it be used?

This chapter is to inform you what end-point assessment (EPA) is about. It is not an assessment approach, but a type of assessment which uses more than one approach to assess a learner at the end of their apprenticeship programme.

End-point assessment relates to the independent summative assessment (sometimes referred to as *synoptic* assessment) of apprenticeship standards. Standards differ for each occupational area which learners might pursue. Summative assessment is undertaken of the learner at the end of their apprenticeship programme. Historically, apprenticeship frameworks included formative assessment, whereas apprenticeship standards now use summative assessment once a learner has completed their training. However, formative assessment can take place during training to ensure progress is being made by the learner. Both formative and summative assessment will take place if the learner is working towards a qualification as part of the apprenticeship standard.

Different apprenticeship standards use a variety of assessment approaches, e.g. practical assessment, interview, project, written and/or multiple-choice questions, tests, exams, product evidence and presentations. The learner must be assessed by a minimum of two different assessment approaches which are most relevant to their occupation. These are mandatory and part of the apprenticeship standard, and must be agreed with the employer and the learner at the start of the programme. This enables the learner to know how they will be assessed.

The learning provider who has been responsible for training the learner is not entitled to undertake the end-point assessment. This must be through an independent organisation that is on the *register of end-point assessment organisations*.

What can it be used for?

End-point assessment is a mandatory element of the apprenticeship standard for a specific occupational area. It is used to test the learner's competence, skills, behaviours, attitudes, knowledge and/or understanding.

If you have been training the learner, you can't influence the summative assessment, but you can ensure your learner is fully prepared. Ensure your learner has plenty of experience by carrying out formative assessment on a regular basis, and providing constructive and developmental feedback. Using an e-portfolio for the learner to upload evidence can make the process easier for all parties involved, as it allows easy access. This enables the employer, as well as the learning provider, to track the learner's progress and agree when the learner is ready for the EPA process.

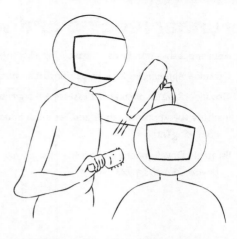

Once the employer and training provider agree that the learner has completed all the mandatory requirements of the apprenticeship standard, and prior to undertaking the EPA, the employer unlocks the *gateway*. The learner can then upload all the mandatory evidence and await instruction from the EPA organisation. An independent assessor from the EPA organisation will then arrange to carry out the required end-point assessment process according to the apprenticeship standard.

Resources

- Resources are provided by the end-point assessment organisation

Advantages

👍 No debt is incurred by the learner as their employer pays for the EPA

👍 An apprenticeship programme provides comprehensive training which leads to a career in a specific occupational area

👍 Assessments are realistic and relate to the learner's job role

Disadvantages

👎 EPA approaches are end-loaded rather than ongoing, and a learner might have forgotten certain aspects by the time they are formally assessed

👎 Learners might become nervous and not perform well during the EPA

👎 If a learner loses their job, they may not be able to complete the apprenticeship programme

---

Tip

To run a very successful apprenticeship programme, a strong tripartite relationship must be developed between the training provider, the employer and the learner, to provide support and enable progression.

Further reading and weblinks

Apprenticeship standards – https://tinyurl.com/yctc7en6

Gov.uk – *Apprenticeships* – https://tinyurl.com/zntft38

Gov.uk – *Register of end-point assessment organisations* – https://tinyurl.com/y58altrd

Institute for Apprenticeships and Technical Education – *Blog: End point assessment* – https://tinyurl.com/y5xg7ntl

Strategic Development Network – *How do you know your apprentice is ready for the gateway?* – https://tinyurl.com/y53gpyx3

9 An essay (or dissertation)

Individual	√	Small group	√	Large group	√
Initial	√	Formative	√	Summative	√
Informal	√	Formal	√	Preparation and marking	√
Entry Level		Level 1 and 2	√	Level 3 upwards	√

What is it and where can it be used?

An essay (or dissertation) is a formal piece of written work produced by the learner based on a relevant topic or subject. It encourages the individual to carry out some independent reading or research. The word *essay* is generally used in secondary and further education, and *dissertation* is used in higher education. An essay usually has a smaller word count than a dissertation.

If you are using an essay as an assessment activity you would firstly design a brief to give to the learners. This would have one or more questions or scenarios as guidance towards meeting the criteria you want your learners to achieve. You should also agree a word-count limit and whether the learner should write in the first person, e.g. if the work is a reflection of their personal experience. Alternatively, it could be in the third person allowing flexibility to demonstrate facts as opposed to personal thoughts. Some awarding organisations provide the brief and word count as part of the assessment criteria, particularly if it is being used as end-point assessment. If you are issuing a dissertation, the learner would usually select the area they want to research and write about it themself, and agree the title and content with you beforehand.

Essays can be set as a homework task or completed during a session, depending on how you are planning to use it. If you are setting it as a homework task, you would need to ensure the work is the learner's own by asking them to sign an authenticity declaration. Dissertations are usually completed in the learner's own time, to enable research to be undertaken, analysed and critically evaluated.

Academic writing and referencing is usually a requirement for level 3 and above qualifications. Further information can be found using the following links: https://tinyurl.com/3684hax and https://tinyurl.com/y2ogv2yp.

What can it be used for?

Essays or dissertations are a great activity to use for summative assessment. They enable the learner to demonstrate the knowledge and understanding they have gained whilst researching and studying a particular aspect of a topic or subject.

They can also be used for formative assessment to measure a learner's progress towards developing the knowledge and understanding required to achieve a qualification.

Essays are a useful activity to use for initial assessment to check whether a learner is suited, able, committed to and/or ready to enrol on a course.

Resources

- The criteria you are wanting your learners to achieve
- Electronic device such as a word processor or pens and paper

Advantages

- Encourages creative-thinking skills
- Can be set to measure a range of levels
- Useful for academic and theoretical subjects
- Supports the development of literacy and language skills

Disadvantages

- Can be time-consuming to mark, assess and provide individual feedback
- Can be subjective when marking
- Plagiarism can be an issue

Tip

If you are setting the essay as a homework task, ensure you give the learners a hand-in date, and tell them what the penalty will be for not submitting on time.

Further reading and weblinks

Gravells A (2016) *Principles and Practices of Assessment*: Learning Matters/SAGE, London.

Mansell S (2019) *50 Teaching and Learning Approaches*: Learning Matters/SAGE, London.

Peoples-uni.org – *Tips on writing assignments* – https://tinyurl.com/jkqh3p7

10   Exit and entry tickets

Individual	√	Small group	√	Large group	*
Initial	√	Formative	√	Summative	
Informal	√	Formal		Preparation and marking	√
Entry Level	√	Level 1 and 2	√	Level 3 upwards	√

*depends upon what and how you are planning to use the approach

What is it and where can it be used?

Exit and entry tickets are about using small pieces of paper or card that learners write on, and then place in a box as they exit or enter a session. To exit a session, learners must write a short statement or sentence about the session they have just attended. To enter a session, learners must write a short statement or sentence about the previous session or a homework task they were set.

This formative assessment approach should take no longer than five minutes. Whether learners are completing exit or entry tickets, they cannot leave or enter the classroom without submitting their answers. If a learner is unable to submit a written answer, you should ask them a question and allow them to give a verbal response.

Learners can write their name on the ticket before submitting, or they can submit anonymously, depending on how you use the approach. You will need to allow yourself time to read the entry tickets. It might be an idea to have an activity the learners can carry out whilst you are doing this. You can read the exit tickets after they have left.

What can it be used for?

Exit tickets are a brilliant formative assessment approach to measure the impact of learning at the end of a topic or subject, or to close the session.

Entry tickets are a wonderful formative assessment approach to measure a learner's prior knowledge and understanding. For example, assessment could be based on a homework task; the content of a previous session; or it could be a question linked to a concept or an idea posed.

Below are some examples of how formative assessment could take place:

- Checking knowledge and understanding – ask learners to write a short statement about the main points they have learnt, or ask them to draw or illustrate their learning.
- Consolidating learning – give learners a problem to solve, or to bullet point the main aspects of their learning.
- Connecting to prior knowledge – ask learners to write a sentence regarding how the current topic links to a previous topic.

- Checking for prior knowledge – ask learners to write what they already know and can do before starting a new topic or subject.

For entry-level learners, an alternative to writing is for them to draw a symbol to demonstrate how they feel about a subject or topic, e.g. a smiley face ☺ to indicate they are happy and have no questions, a neutral face ☺ to indicate they are unsure, or a sad face ☹ to indicate they don't understand something.

Ideally, learners will add their names to the statements/ symbols. If you use this approach anonymously, it is difficult to know if an individual is struggling, or if they have misinterpreted any part of the session. If names are included this allows you to follow up any concerns on an individual basis.

Resources

- Paper or card and pens (sticky notes or electronic devices could also be used)
- A box in which to post the completed tickets

Advantages

👍 Can help to measure an individual's progress

👍 Supports the development of critical-thinking skills

👍 Encourages quiet or less confident learners to engage with the subject

👍 Versatile approach which can be adapted to suit individual or group needs

Disadvantages

👎 Some learners may not take it seriously

👎 Can be time-consuming to read through all the comments

Tip

You can use this approach to evaluate your own performance. Ask learners to complete an exit ticket by writing or drawing an image to indicate how well they felt the session went.

Further reading and weblinks

TeachBeyond – *Exit slip: Your ticket to closure* – https://tinyurl.com/y43t2uje

Theteacherstoolkit – *Exit ticket* – https://tinyurl.com/nbxej5a

11 Holistic assessment

Individual	√	Small group	√	Large group	
Initial	√	Formative	√	Summative	√
Informal	√	Formal	√	Preparation and marking	*
Entry Level	√	Level 1 and 2	√	Level 3 upwards	√

*depends upon what and how you are planning to use the approach

What is it and where can it be used?

Holistic assessment enables learners to demonstrate several aspects of a programme or qualification's criteria at the same time. It can be formal or informal and used for vocational or academic qualifications. For example, if a learner is undertaking a vocational qualification, an holistic assessment of a practical task could include observing customer services, selecting and handling tools and equipment, working with others, and health and safety. If a learner is undertaking an academic qualification, they might have written a reflective learning log which could be assessed holistically, demonstrating evidence of competency as well as knowledge. The achievements would need to be cross-referenced to the criteria.

Holistic assessment can be used anywhere which allows a learner to undertake an assessment activity. If planned correctly, it can capture competence, skills, behaviours, attitudes, knowledge and/or understanding in one task.

What can it be used for?

Holistic assessment can be used at the initial assessment stage to ascertain a learner's level of knowledge and/or competency towards a topic or subject. It can be used as part of ongoing teaching and learning through formative assessment to measure a learner's progress. It can also be used as part of a learner's evidence base through summative assessment. This would enable the assessor to make a professional judgement of achievement towards certain outcomes. For example, a learner undertaking a Level 2 Nail Technology qualification must not only complete a health and safety unit, they must also demonstrate health and safety in all the other units. By using holistic assessment, the learner can provide evidence across more than one unit, rather than repeating the same or a similar assessment activity again.

Resources

- Depends on the topic or subject being assessed

Advantages

- Cost-effective
- Time-saving
- Covers more than one outcome
- Can increase attainment
- Helps learners link knowledge to practice

Disadvantages

- Can become complicated if not planned carefully
- Can confuse some learners if the criteria to be assessed are not clear or not planned for
- Can be time-consuming and difficult to cross-reference towards the assessment criteria

---

Tip

When planning to use holistic assessment, ensure the learner's evidence meets the full criteria of all the outcomes which have been planned to be assessed. If it doesn't, identify and consider the best method to capture any missing evidence.

Further reading and weblinks

Gravells A (2016) *Principles and Practices of Assessment*: Learning Matters/SAGE, London.

Greer et al. (2019) *The Vocational Assessor Handbook*: Kogan Page, London.

12 Interview

Individual	√	Small group		Large group	
Initial	√	Formative	√	Summative	
Informal	√	Formal	√	Preparation and marking	√
Entry Level	√	Level 1 and 2	√	Level 3 upwards	√

What is it and where can it be used?

Interviews are a one-to-one conversation or a discussion between an assessor and a learner. They are usually before the commencement of a learning programme to ensure the right programme is chosen. This can be formal or informal but the dialogue or any questions used should be consistent. However, the line of questioning may change depending on the learner's needs. For example, you could ask all learners (on an individual basis) if they have a particular need, e.g. a learning difficulty and/or a disability. If a learner discloses this, the line of questioning would change to enable you to ascertain their needs, and to agree how you can support them.

Interviews can take place face-to-face, using a telephone or through online media. They usually last up to 60 minutes.

Interviews can be incorporated into reviews of progress, formal questioning and/or professional discussions to assess ongoing progress and achievement.

What can it be used for?

Interviews are a fantastic assessment approach to establish a learner's starting point. It is beneficial if a learner completes an application form prior to the interview, determining their learning programme preference, previous learning, qualifications, any work experience, career aspirations and goals, any learning needs or financial hardships which may affect their ability to learn or attend sessions. Using the information provided on the application form can save time. It can enable you to effectively plan the interview, to question the learner further in terms of identifying the correct level and learning programme for them. Initial assessment and a skills scan (see Chapter 38) can also be used alongside the interview to help identify a learner's starting point.

Resources

- Depends on the method used for interview, i.e. face to face, telephone or media
- A pro-forma to document, or an electronic device, to record the learner's responses
- Pre-prepared interview questions

Advantages

👍 Supports establishing what a learner already knows and can do

👍 Gives the assessor the opportunity to get to know the individual

👍 Identifies the learner's aspirations and/or goals

👍 Informs initial target setting

Disadvantages

👎 Can be time-consuming

👎 Not all learners will be truthful during the interview, or will want to disclose some personal aspects

👎 Some learners may be nervous and not fully engage in the process

👎 Difficult to standardise and requires careful planning

Tip

To help your learner relax, you could start by asking them about any interests or hobbies they have. To encourage them to engage freely in conversation, you should use open body language, i.e. by using eye contact and not folding your arms.

Further reading and weblinks

Gravells A (2016) *Principles and Practice of Assessment*: Learning Matters/SAGE, London.

Petty G (2009) *Evidence-based Teaching: A Practical Approach* (2nd edn): Cheltenham, Nelson Thornes.

13   Learner demonstration

Individual	√	Small group	√	Large group	√
Initial	√	Formative	√	Summative	√
Informal	√	Formal	√	Preparation and marking	*
Entry Level	√	Level 1 and 2	√	Level 3 upwards	√

depends upon what and how you are planning to use the approach

What is it and where can it be used?

Learner demonstration is an assessment approach which captures evidence of a learner's competence, skills, behaviours, attitudes, knowledge and/or understanding. It can be physical, visual or auditory, for example using: projects; presentations; spoken words; multimedia; works of art; music; drama; dance; sports activities; essays; digital media; experiments and reports.

What can it be used for?

Learner demonstration can be used formally or informally to assess a practical task. It helps to assess that the learner has gained the required knowledge and understanding to perform the task correctly. It's a superb assessment approach for formative assessment as it enables you to measure a learner's progress. For example, a group of learners studying Level 2 Media Make Up are learning how to produce a *day look* for which they will be summatively assessed in a few weeks' time. The assessor asks the group to work in pairs and to create a *smoky eye look*. The learners start by using colour charts to visually demonstrate the colours they will use before physically demonstrating on each other.

The assessor can observe and formatively assess each pair, providing informal feedback to help them improve their practice, prior to the summative assessment. In addition, if learners are working in pairs or small groups they could peer assess each other (see Chapter 21).

Learner demonstration is also a fantastic approach for summative assessment. For example, part of the summative assessment of a first-aid course requires learners to demonstrate how they would deal with an accident scenario with more than one casualty. They must also recognise any health and safety issues which could put them in danger, and deal with the casualties in the right order, with those with life-threatening injuries being dealt with first. A learner can physically demonstrate how they would deal with the scenario by attending to the casualties. Alternatively, they can demonstrate visually using a flip chart or electronic presentation, along with a spoken commentary.

Learner demonstration can also be used during initial assessment to ascertain a learner's starting point.

Resources

- Equipment and resources (if it's a practical demonstration)
- Flip chart paper, posters or a computer and projector if it's a visual demonstration

Advantages

👍 Helps the learners to develop confidence and improve their communication skills

👍 Interactive and learner centred

👍 Helps to develop problem solving and independent thinking skills

Disadvantages

👎 Can become disorganised (if with a large group)

👎 Can be heavily reliant on resources and equipment

👎 Can be time-consuming to organise

👎 A time limit must be agreed and adhered to, otherwise the learner might over-run

👎 If it's a group demonstration, individual learner contributions must be assessed

---

Tip

When planning to use learner demonstration, ensure it is purposeful and meaningful, and not designed as a show and tell activity or just to fill in time.

Further reading and weblinks

Mansell S (2019) *50 Teaching and Learning Approaches*: Learning Matters/SAGE, London.

Petty G (2009) *Evidence-based Teaching: A Practical Approach* (2nd edn): Cheltenham, Nelson Thornes.

The Glossary of Education Reform – *Demonstration of learning* – https://tinyurl.com/y6bkvtx4

14 Learner statement

Individual	√	Small group	√	Large group	√
Initial	*	Formative	√	Summative	√
Informal	√	Formal	√	Preparation and marking	√
Entry Level	√	Level 1 and 2	√	Level 3 upwards	√

*depends upon what and how you are planning to use the approach

What is it and where can it be used?

A learner statement is a factual account, written by the learner, of what they have done. It is usually related to competency-based outcomes.

The learner statement should be factual and detail the actions they have undertaken to complete a task, or use it to state how they handled a particular situation or issue. For example, a learner studying Level 2 Animal Care must feed a range of animals. Their learner statement would detail or list the steps they took to feed each individual animal. This could be supported with photographic evidence, or a witness testimony from their supervisor.

It can be used anywhere that a learner is able to access the resources and equipment to undertake a relevant task.

What can it be used for?

A learner statement can be formal or informal. It can be used for formative assessment to help improve a learner's performance or summative assessment to help confirm their achievements. It differs from a reflective log (see Chapter 32) as the learner only documents the actions they have taken, rather than how they could improve. However, the learner could be encouraged to reflect on their statement after the event.

A learner statement is an effective summative assessment approach when additional evidence is required to support an assessment decision. For example, a learner may have been observed by an assessor carrying out a practical task and deemed as competent. However, the assessment criteria may require evidence of the learner carrying out the task more than once, and this is where a learner statement could be used.

Resources

- Depends upon what and how you are planning to use the approach

Advantages

👍 Improves written work

👍 Can help improve a learner's performance (if used formatively)

👍 Can be motivational as it helps the learner to take ownership of their achievements

Disadvantages

👎 Must be planned thoroughly to ensure the learner is documenting the correct factual information

👎 Can only be used as additional evidence by the learner, as the assessor must confirm competence for summative assessment

👎 Can be time-consuming to mark and assess

👎 Learners might write too much, or too little

Tip

A learner statement template with heading and subheadings, or a table for them to complete, will support new learners to document the factual evidence required. Stating a word count will help focus the learner's writing.

Further reading and weblinks

Gravells A (2016) *Principles and Practices of Assessment*: Learning Matters/SAGE, London.

15 Listening tests

Individual	√	Small group	√	Large group	
Initial	√	Formative	√	Summative	√
Informal	√	Formal	√	Preparation and marking	√
Entry Level	√	Level 1 and 2	√	Level 3 upwards	√

What is it and where can it be used?

A listening test is an assessment approach intended to measure a learner's knowledge and understanding of what they hear. If the listening test is being used informally, it can usually be undertaken in any appropriate environment. If it is being used formally, an official area must be set up, and invigilators used to oversee the process to ensure learners are not communicating with anyone, and that it is fair for all. Most formal listening tests have a limited amount of time for the learners to complete them, however not all learners will complete within the time. Some awarding organisations stipulate the date a formal test or examination must be taken, with a start and end time, e.g. GCSE French Higher Tier, Paper 1: Listening, is currently allocated 35 minutes.

What can it be used for?

Listening tests are a good way to assess the progress your learners are making towards their targets in specific subjects, such as music or languages. They enable you to formatively measure knowledge and comprehension, and can be used throughout a programme of study either formally or informally. For example, a learner who is going to be taking a GCSE formal music exam could practise by undertaking mock tests. The learner will be assessed on their listening and contextual understanding. The mock test could include listening exercises and written questions using music excerpts.

Listening tests can also be used to measure how well a learner or a small group of learners can remember and follow a set of verbal instructions. For example, you might ask a small group of learners to carry out a health and safety risk assessment of a carpentry workshop. The verbal instruction could include details of what tools and equipment are to be risk assessed, the reason for the risk assessment and who it should include. Or an individual learner could be given verbal instructions to complete a set of tasks in a particular sequence. The progress measures for both examples are whether the learners have remembered and retained the verbal instruction, and completed the full task in the correct sequence and time.

Listening tests are regularly used for those who are learning a different language from their own, e.g. English for Speakers of Other Languages (ESOL) includes summative assessment regarding listening skills as part of the speaking and listening unit.

Listening tests can also be used as part of the initial assessment process to measure a learner's knowledge and understanding. This will support you in advising them which qualification and level they should work towards.

Resources

- Sound for the listening test content
- A device for the learner to use to hear the sound (if not given in person)
- Pens and paper or access to an electronic device if written answers are required
- An area which can be adjusted to meet any examination conditions

Advantages

👍 Can help to develop employability skills

👍 A handy way to regularly check progress

👍 Encourages learners to focus on their listening skills

Disadvantages

👎 Can be time-consuming and difficult to create (if designing your own test)

👎 Learners may get anxious and perhaps not perform to their best ability

👎 Not suitable for learners who are hard of hearing

Tip

Start with an easy task and just a few instructions to enable the learner to develop their listening and sequencing skills, before making the task harder. This will help to measure how well a learner can listen to and follow a set of instructions.

Further reading and weblinks

Beals G and Edwards J (2003) *Listening Skills: Years 5/6 and P6/7 Bk.3*: Prim-Ed Publishing Ltd, Wexford.

Conti G and Smith S (2019) *Breaking the Sound Barrier: Teaching Language Learners How to Listen*: independently published.

Rickerby S and Lanbett S (1999) *Listening Skills: Key Stage 1*: Questions Publishing Company Ltd, Birmingham.

16 Multiple-choice questions

Individual	√	Small group	√	Large group	√
Initial	√	Formative	√	Summative	√
Informal	√	Formal	√	Preparation and marking	*
Entry Level	√	Level I and 2	√	Level 3 upwards	√

depends upon what and how you are planning to use the approach

What is it and where can it be used?

Multiple-choice questions are a question-type test which requires learners to select the correct answer from one or more possible answers. They are made up of two parts, a question (known as the *stem*) followed by one or more correct answers (known as the *key/keys*) and two or three incorrect answers (known as *distractors*). Multiple-choice tests can be assessed manually, or assessed automatically via specialist software, depending on how you need to use the test.

Some awarding organisations supply ready-made multiple-choice questions. These are either marked by the assessor or marked online.

There are several ways to create multiple-choice questions if you need to write your own. However, answers and distracters should always be similar in length and complexity (or be words, diagrams or pictures).

Learners could be given a question and asked to select one correct answer out of four possible answers. For example, a learner studying Level 2 Plumbing could be asked:

Which cutter can be used to cut metallic or plastic pipes?

a) Rotary cutter

b) Fly cutter

c) Tube cutter

d) Slotting cutter

The answer is c.

Alternatively, learners could be given a question and asked to select three or four correct answers from a list. Another example for Level 2 Plumbing could be:

Select the three words which best describe a washer:

a) Square

b) Round

c) Flat

d) Disk

e) Long

The answer is b, c and d.

When writing questions, you need to take into account the level of learning you are assessing, the terminology used, and the complexity of the language you are using. For example, short questions with one-word answers are appropriate for level 1, and longer questions and responses with more complex wording are appropriate for higher levels.

What can it be used for?

Multiple-choice questions can be used formatively to measure a learner's progress and check their memory and recall skills. They can be included at the end of a topic or subject as a summative assessment to test a learner's knowledge and understanding. If they are used formally, they should be given under exam conditions. Alternatively, they can form part of the initial assessment process to find out how much a learner already knows and understands about a topic.

To aid standardisation, a bank of questions can be built up by several assessors in a team. The questions can then be randomly chosen to create different versions of the test for different learners.

Resources

- Multiple-choice questions
- Paper and pens or a computer/internet connection with relevant software

Advantages

- Questions are quick and easy to mark
- Can be used for a wide range of subject content
- Can be used more than once with different learners

Disadvantages

- Can be time-consuming to create
- Learners could guess the correct answer
- Do not support learners to develop understanding, only test a learner's recall or knowledge

Tip

During a session, it can be beneficial for learners to write a few multiple-choice questions and responses to test the rest of the group. This gives them an insight into how the questions are formulated, and how thoroughly they need to read and understand what the question is asking, before choosing a response.

Further reading and weblinks

Gravells A (2016) *Principles and Practices of Assessment*: Learning Matters/SAGE, London.

Mansell S (2019) *50 Teaching and Learning Approaches*: Learning Matters/SAGE, London.

University of Waterloo – *Designing multiple-choice questions* – https://tinyurl.com/kwjyzoo

17 Naturally occurring evidence

Individual	√	Small group	√	Large group	
Initial		Formative	√	Summative	√
Informal	√	Formal	√	Preparation and marking	*
Entry Level	√	Level 1 and 2	√	Level 3 upwards	√

*depends upon what and how you are planning to use the approach

What is it and where can it be used?

Naturally occurring evidence is a way of observing a learner when a real situation, job or task is taking place, usually in their workplace. For example, a learner undertaking a Level 2 Motor Mechanic qualification may have the opportunity to service a customer's vehicle. Careful planning with the learner and their employer should enable you to agree dates and times of when is best to go into the workplace to carry out the assessment.

Planning for naturally occurring evidence should take place at the beginning of a learner taking a qualification or working towards a standard. However, there are occasions when naturally occurring evidence presents itself which has not been pre-planned or agreed with the learner. These opportunities should not be discounted as they can form some wonderful complementary evidence towards a learner meeting the requirements.

What can it be used for?

Using naturally occurring evidence as an assessment approach is a fabulous way for a learner to demonstrate their competence, skills, behaviours, attitudes, knowledge and/or understanding. A formal observation of a learner undertaking a practical task in the workplace would form great evidence for summative assessment. Don't forget to ask questions to ensure the learner also has the required understanding.

Naturally occurring evidence may arise at any time and can't always be planned for; sometimes it may not be possible for a formal assessment to take place. In such cases, informal assessment could be used, e.g. a reflective log, a witness testimony, photographic or video evidence which can be supportive and additional to the other evidence already gathered. Additional informal evidence must be cross-referenced to the assessment criteria to enable formal assessment and quality assurance to take place.

Naturally occurring evidence can also be used as a formative assessment approach to enable the learner to gain valuable feedback to help improve their performance, e.g. a learner may be able to complete a job or task, but not within industry timings, and they are therefore deemed as not yet competent.

Resources

- Tools or equipment relevant to the job or task

Advantages

- Can be motivating to the learner
- Can meet more than one assessment criteria
- Can support critical-thinking and problem-solving skills
- Is accepted by most awarding organisations
- The evidence can be left in its natural location for the assessor to view

Disadvantages

- Is time-consuming to plan for and cross-reference
- Can be difficult to standardise practice, i.e. of different assessors' decisions
- Difficult to manage with more than one learner

Tip

Naturally occurring evidence must not be used as a replacement for well-planned evidence collection. It should be formally assessed and used as a source of complementary or additional evidence.

Further reading and weblinks

Training Qualifications UK – *What is off-the-job-training?* – https://tinyurl.com/y6znaopr

18 Observation

Individual	√	Small group	√	Large group	*
Initial	√	Formative	√	Summative	√
Informal	√	Formal	√	Preparation and marking	*
Entry Level	√	Level 1 and 2	√	Level 3 upwards	√

*depends upon what and how you are planning to use the approach

What is it and where can it be used?

Observation is about watching a learner perform a task to see if they have the ability to competently complete it to the specific assessment criteria. Observation for a summative assessment should be planned with the learner to allow them time to practise and prepare. You will need to agree where the observation will take place, e.g. a learner undertaking a qualification in Level 2 Motor Mechanics could be observed in the workplace or a realistic working environment, or even be visually recorded for the assessor to view later. The qualification specification will identify where the observation should take place and by who.

The assessment plan should include exactly what will be assessed including any holistic assessment (see Chapter 11) and approximately how long the assessment will take. This ensures the assessor and the learner focus on what is needed to meet the assessment criteria, and if any additional evidence is required such as oral questioning or via a professional discussion (see Chapters 20 and 27).

The learner's performance should be documented by the assessor, either electronically or by note taking, writing concise comments towards the assessment criteria. It is vital that each learner experiences the same controlled conditions wherever the assessment is taking place and who observes it.

What can it be used for?

Observation is typically used for assessing practical skills but may also be used during group work to monitor how much input each learner has had. It's a fantastic tool to measure progress in a formative informal setting to identify any skills' gaps in competence, behaviours, attitudes, knowledge and/or understanding. This would enable you to give developmental advice and support.

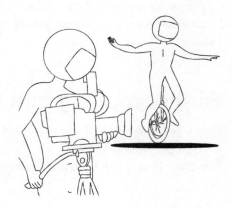

Observation is often used during initial assessment as part of a skills scan (see Chapter 38), e.g. a learner planning to study Level 3 Make-up Artistry could be asked to complete a *trade test* to demonstrate their competency prior to being enrolled.

Observation is also a very popular activity for summative assessment to ensure the learner has met all the required criteria.

Resources

- Paper and pen or an electronic device to document/record the learner's achievements
- Depends on the area of study as to what physical resources are required

Advantages

- A brilliant way to assess a learner's practical skills
- Reliable and authentic as you are observing the learner carrying out the task
- Can holistically assess several aspects of a programme or a qualification at the same time
- Results are immediate
- Easy to identify any skills' gaps

Disadvantages

- Can be time-consuming to plan and assess
- Does not always capture the full assessment requirements, therefore additional observations or evidence will be required
- Learners can become shy or anxious and not perform as well as usual
- Can be difficult to standardise practice, i.e. of different assessors' decisions

---

Tip

Ensure the learner is fully involved in the planning process for summative assessment, to enable them to prepare physically and mentally.

Further reading and weblinks

Chan C (2009) *Assessment: Direct Observation*: University of Hong Kong, Assessment Resources@ HKU [http://ar.cetl.hku.hk].

Ollin R and Tucker J (2019) *The Vocational Assessor Handbook*: London, Kogan Page.

19 Online assessment

Individual	√	Small group	√	Large group	√
Initial	√	Formative	√	Summative	√
Informal	√	Formal	√	Preparation and marking	*
Entry Level	√	Level 1 and 2	√	Level 3 upwards	√

depends upon what and how you are planning to use the approach

What is it and where can it be used?

Online assessment is the term used to describe different types of tests, exams, assignments or portfolio work undertaken using an electronic device. It is also known as e-assessment, e-portfolio, gateway assessment (for end-point assessment) or onscreen assessment.

It can be used anywhere that an electronic device can be accessed. Depending on the planned assessment method, it may be necessary to have an internet connection, and to password protect the online access.

The learner will need to produce identification to prove who they are, e.g. if the assessor has never met the learner prior to the test.

What can it be used for?

Online assessment is a flexible method which can be used for a range of assessment types, e.g. an initial assessment to determine a learner's mathematical skills, followed by a diagnostic test to see which areas a learner needs to develop. This could be followed up, after several teaching and learning sessions, with a formative online assessment to measure progress. The learner would complete the cycle by undertaking an online summative examination.

Online assessment doesn't have to be all about formal tests or examinations. It can be used informally to develop or measure a learner's competence, skills, behaviours, attitudes, knowledge and/or understanding of a particular topic or subject. Multiple-choice questions could be used online (see Chapter 16).

Depending on the qualification or programme of learning a learner is undertaking, online assessment could be used to build up evidence

of their work through an e-portfolio. This is where learners upload proof of how they have met the assessment criteria, e.g. a learner undertaking Level 2 Countryside Management could upload photographs of a particular task they have carried out with an explanation against each, detailing what they are doing and why. Note that you would need to be careful regarding the authenticy of the learner's work if you have not witnessed them carrying it out.

Digital technology software can be used to randomly select questions, and electronically mark and grade some online tests and exams. This ensures all tests are marked to the same standard, and saves the assessor a lot of time. Other software allows e-marking, where the assessor accesses and assesses the evidence which a learner has uploaded.

Resources

- A suitable electronic device (with an internet connection if required)
- Software to support the assessment approach

Advantages

- Once set up it can save a lot of time as the questions can be used again
- Multiple learners can undertake the assessment at the same time, or at different times if the questions are randomly selected by the online system
- Results are usually immediate

Disadvantages

- Learners need to be able to use a computer or an appropriate electronic device
- Technology and internet connections are not always reliable
- Can be expensive to initially set up
- Technical support might be needed
- If set as a homework task, it can be difficult to know if it is the learner's own work (an authenticity declaration could be signed by the learner)

Tip

Plan to use a wide range of informal online assessment approaches with your learners. This will enable them to grow their confidence and skills at using online assessments.

Further reading and weblinks

Atherton P (2018) *50 Ways to Use Technology Enhanced Learning in the Classroom*: Learning Matters/ SAGE, London.

Bryan C (2019) *Innovative Assessment in Higher Education* (2nd edn): Routledge, London.

Mansell S (2019) *50 Teaching and Learning Approaches*: Learning Matters/SAGE, London.

SDN – *How do you know your apprentice is ready for the gateway?* – https://tinyurl.com/y53gpyx3

White J (2019) *Digital Literacy Skills for FE Teachers*: Learning Matters/SAGE, London.

20 Oral questioning

Individual	√	Small group	√	Large group	√
Initial	√	Formative	√	Summative	√
Informal	√	Formal	√	Preparation and marking	√
Entry Level	√	Level 1 and 2	√	Level 3 upwards	√

What is it and where can it be used?

Oral questioning is about asking open questions directly to an individual to check their competence, knowledge, understanding, attitudes and to stimulate thinking. An example of an open question is: *What is the difference between short crust pastry and flaky pastry?* An open question must not allow a learner to answer by saying *yes* or *no*. An easy way to remember how to do this is to start a question with *who, what, when, where, why* or *how.*

What can it be used for?

Oral questioning, when used well, is a great way to assess an individual's knowledge, attitudes and understanding which could be an *initial, formative* or *summative* type of assessment. The most important aspect of asking a question is knowing the individual learner in terms of their starting point. Some learners may already have a certain amount of knowledge regarding a subject, whereas others don't. An assessor who knows their group will be able to ask relevant questions that stretch and challenge individuals, and measure their progress in a formal setting. It's also a fantastic tool to use in a taught session to refocus and reengage individuals, or to bring the whole group back together after an activity.

In an informal setting, questions should range from easy to hard. You could start by asking an easy question and when the learner answers correctly, build on their answer by asking another question. By using initial assessment, you will know learners' starting points, and careful tracking of their individual progress throughout the programme will give you a measure of where those learners are in terms of the topic or subject. Questioning enables you to pose a question to an individual at the correct level for them, allowing them to demonstrate the progress they have made.

In a formal setting, oral questioning is a brilliant method to gather missing or further evidence towards summative assessment. When collating evidence for summative assessment it is useful to write down the learner's answers or to use a device which can record them.

Oral questioning enables you to pose a question to an individual at the correct level for them, allowing them to demonstrate what they know and can do well.

Resources

- A bank of relevant open questions
- Paper and pen or a device to record responses if using the activity for summative assessment

Advantages

- Enables the learner to think about what they are learning
- Challenges a learner's potential
- An effective way of testing knowledge and understanding
- Refocuses groups
- Reengages individuals
- Can be used in a wide variety of ways to suit individual needs (particularly when you are teaching groups at different levels during the same session)

Disadvantages

- Questions must be well planned to meet individual needs and enable stretch and challenge to take place
- Questions must be open, otherwise you will only gain a *yes* or *no* response which doesn't demonstrate knowledge or understanding
- Questions must be unambiguous
- Difficult to manage with a large group of learners, as can be quite time-consuming to ensure there are enough questions to allow each learner to have a go at answering
- Some learners may shout out and try to answer questions (if asked to the group without nominating a learner's name who will answer)
- A shy or nervous learner may not engage well during the session, as they could struggle to provide an answer in front of their peers

---

Tip

When using oral questioning in an informal setting, call out the learner's name prior to asking the question, as this will help prevent others from shouting the answer. Learners who have already answered their question may become disengaged.

(Continued)

(Continued)

Use this technique at different points during the session, rather than asking all the questions at the same point.

If you have a small group, you could ask the same learner more than one question to ensure they remain engaged.

Further reading and weblinks

Gravells A (2017) *Principles and Practices of Teaching and Training*: Learning Matters/SAGE, London.

Mansell S (2019) *50 Teaching and Learning Approaches*: Learning Matters/SAGE, London.

Petty G – *Improve your teaching and that of your team* – https://tinyurl.com/lqusrxe

Teaching and Learning Guru – *Asking students the right questions* – https://tinyurl.com/ya7wuzvr

21 Peer assessment

Individual		Small group	√	Large group		√
Initial	*	Formative	√	Summative		
Informal	√	Formal		Preparation and marking		
Entry Level		Level 1 and 2	√	Level 3 upwards		√

*depends upon what and how you are planning to use the approach

What is it and where can it be used?

Peer assessment is a collaborative approach which involves the learners assessing each other's work after an activity. Clear assessment criteria must be shared with, and explained to, the learners. They must follow these to assess the activity and to provide feedback to their peers. The main purpose of peer assessment is to encourage learners to take responsibility for their own learning. They must fully engage in the process and understand the assessment criteria to be able to participate.

Peer assessment could include many aspects of a learner's work, e.g. written work, product evidence, presentation, or a practical activity. This enables learners to see and learn from each other, e.g. a learner would peer assess a good piece of written work and decide to use similar strategies for their future work, or they may see a poor piece of work and use the experience to improve the work they are doing.

What can it be used for?

Peer assessment is a fantastic approach for formative assessment it can be used as an individual or a group approach. For example, a group of learners could be given a topic to present back to their peers. Individually, each learner would present their topic, and at the end of their presentation their peers would provide feedback. Alternatively, learners could be placed into pairs and asked to peer assess each other's product evidence following a specific assessment activity.

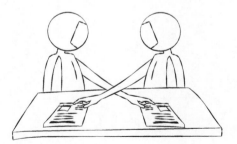

Resources

*   The specific assessment or marking criteria

Advantages

👍 Encourages learner involvement and responsibility

👍 Provides additional and relevant feedback

👍 Promotes communication and interaction between peers

Disadvantages

👎 Learners might not assess fairly (for fear of upsetting their peers)

👎 Must be managed well to avoid peer conflict

👎 Not all learners will engage in the process

Tip

To help prevent conflict, ensure the learners fully understand the assessment criteria, and how to provide constructive feedback to their peers.

Further reading and weblinks

Gravells A (2016) *Principles and Practices of Assessment*: Learning Matters/SAGE, London.

TES – *Peer-assessment ideas for secondary students* – https://tinyurl.com/y3vyfa72

Tummons J (2011) *Assessing Learning in the Lifelong Learning Sector*: Learning Matters, Exeter.

University of Reading – *Engage in assessment* – https://tinyurl.com/y683sagu

22   Photographic testimony

Individual	√	Small group	√	Large group	
Initial		Formative	√	Summative	√
Informal	√	Formal	√	Preparation and marking time	√
Entry Level	√	Level 1 and 2	√	Level 3 upwards	√

What is it and where can it be used?

A photographic testimony is compiled by a learner to show their achievements. It is proof of them demonstrating a practical task whilst photographs are taken, and should include images of any tools and/or equipment used. The images should be downloaded or copied and pasted into a grid or template. The grid or template should allow a space for each of the photographs to be sequenced in the order the task was undertaken. There should be enough room for the learner to include a written explanation under each photograph which states what they are doing and why. For example, a learner studying a Level 2 Motor Mechanic qualification must demonstrate they can carry out an oil change on a car. They would take photographs of:

- the job card
- the car
- a screenshot of the information they access on a computer such as the type and amount of oil and filter required
- the ramp to lift the car
- the car on the ramp

They would then continue to take photographs of what they were doing, including any car parts they have removed and replaced, as well as the tools and equipment used.

Under each of the photographs, they should explain what is represented and how it meets the qualification criteria, including any legal or health and safety considerations.

What can it be used for?

A photographic testimony can be used as a formative or summative assessment approach. It is ideal to use as supplementary evidence to a witness testimony, a learner statement, or to support an observation in the workplace.

The photographic testimony could form part of a formal portfolio of evidence or an assignment, or be used informally for the assessor to provide feedback to the learner regarding their progress. Authenticy of the learner carrying out the task must be proved.

Alternatively, during a session, learners in small groups could take pictures of each other carrying out a task, and compile a visual record to present to the full group.

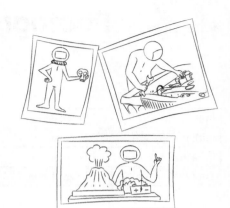

Resources

- A digital camera (e.g. a mobile phone with a built-in camera)
- Access to the internet
- Relevant computer software
- Digital storage device to save the images

Advantages

👍 Develops computer skills

👍 Develops problem-solving and critical-thinking skills

👍 Encourages sequencing

👍 Encourages independent thinking skills

👍 Can help to identify skills gaps

Disadvantages

👎 Learners need access to relevant devices and a digital camera

👎 Learners could focus on the creative aspect and not on the content

👎 Assessment can be subjective

👎 The assessor must confirm the learner did actually do what they are claiming

👎 Not all learners will take it seriously

Tip

Some of the photographs may have to be taken by someone else to allow the image to show that the learner really is carrying out the task. In addition, learners must be carrying out the task naturally and not posing for the camera.

Further reading and weblinks

Education and Training Foundation Excellence Gateway – *A RARPA photographic evidence sheet* – https://tinyurl.com/yyghu5p7

The Open University – *Putting together a portfolio of evidence* – https://tinyurl.com/y5hzzsey

23 Portfolio or e-portfolio

Individual	√	Small group	√	Large group	√
Initial		Formative	√	Summative	√
Informal	√	Formal	√	Preparation and marking	√
Entry Level	√	Level 1 and 2	√	Level 3 upwards	√

What is it and where can it be used?

A portfolio or e-portfolio is a formal record of evidence produced by a learner, towards their qualification or programme of learning. It can be paper-based or electronic depending on the available resources within your organisation and/or any awarding organisation requirements. If you are using an electronic version known as an e-portfolio, it can be accessed via an electronic device by the learner and assessor, in any location where there is an internet connection. A paper-based portfolio has to be manually carried from one place to another.

What can it be used for?

Portfolios are a great way for learners who don't like formal examinations to produce evidence at their own pace. It can be quite motivational for a learner due to the visibility of the evidence. Gathering the evidence is a developmental process which allows learners to demonstrate via a range of activities how they have met the qualification or programme criteria, e.g. a learner studying Level 1 Land Based Operations could have a wide range of evidence including photographs, with explanations of the tasks undertaken, a work log, observation records from their assessor, worksheets, records of question-and-answer sheets, and witness testimonies.

The work produced by the learner can be assessed formatively to help them develop further, prior to formal assessment. Alternatively, it can be used towards the final summative assessment. You should always provide detailed feedback (which can be included in the portfolio) explaining what the learner needs to do to achieve the requirements. Feedback can also reflect how they can improve their practice to develop higher-level skills, when they have achieved the required outcomes.

Each item of evidence should be cross-referenced to all the relevant criteria. This would enable one piece of evidence to meet different outcomes across several units. If you are using a paper-based version, the evidence will need to be manually cross-referenced to the criteria. Generally, an e-portfolio automatically cross-references the evidence for the learner if they upload it in the correct online area.

Resources

- An electronic device and internet connection or paper, pens and a file to keep the paper documents in

Advantages

👍 Can be completed over a period of time

👍 Learner centred

👍 Promotes independent skills and creativity

👍 Promotes organisational skills

👍 A wide variety of assessment activities can be used to generate evidence

👍 Learners can use their portfolio as a point of reference after the assessment has taken place

Disadvantages

👎 Can be time-consuming to assess

👎 Learners tend to produce a large quantity of evidence which is not always relevant

👎 Open to plagiarism

👎 Can be subjective between assessors

👎 Learners can spend too much time on the layout rather than the content

---

Tip

If using a paper-based portfolio, encourage learners to keep their notes and any handouts in a separate file. It's quality that counts not quantity.

Further reading and weblinks

Gravells A (2016) *Principles and Practices of Assessment*: Learning Matters/SAGE, London.

Jisk – *Getting started with e-portfolios* – https://tinyurl.com/hhltjzc

24 Presentation

Individual	√	Small group	√	Large group	*
Initial		Formative	√	Summative	√
Informal	√	Formal	√	Preparation and marking	*
Entry Level		Level I and 2	√	Level 3 upwards	√

*depends upon what and how you are planning to use the approach

What is it and where can it be used?

A presentation gives the learners the opportunity to research a question or a particular subject, and then present their findings to you (and their peer group if applicable). It could be based on the qualification's assessment criteria or a relevant topic, e.g. a learner produces slides and notes using relevant software and then presents it to you/the group. The research for the presentation can form part of the class time but is better set as a homework task to give learners ample time to prepare.

The presentation should be no longer than 20 minutes, and five minutes should be allowed for questions at the end. Assessment is carried out via your observation of the presentation and how well your learner responds to your questioning. If you are using presentations for summative assessment, the learner should hand in a copy of their presentation and any notes they have used for you to assess. You will need to ensure the work is the learner's own by asking them to sign an authenticity declaration.

Depending on the group size, learners can present individually, in pairs or in small groups. If learners are presenting in pairs or small groups, you may need to ask questions if you are unable to ascertain how much input each learner has made towards the research.

You could give additional tasks to those learners who have not clearly demonstrated the required criteria. However, the tasks must be produced in a way which measures the required criteria, be completed within a set time frame, and follow all awarding organisation requirements for assessment and feedback.

What can it be used for?

Presentations are a great way for learners to demonstrate and summarise what they know and understand, in a formal setting. By observing their presentation and asking questions at the end, you can assess their behaviours, attitudes, knowledge and understanding. In addition, you can assess the content of their slides and any written notes, to provide feedback and to further develop each individual.

Presentations can also be used in an informal setting, e.g. asking the learners to carry out a short presentation regarding what they already know about a particular subject or topic. This will enable you to gain an insight into each learner's starting point. External subject experts could be invited to the session to observe the presentation and provide feedback. However, if you are using the presentation as a formal assessment approach, you would need to assess the presentation yourself to make a final decision.

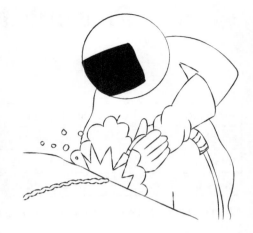

If using presentation as a formal assessment approach, learners will need to be given clear timings as to when their presentation is going to take place and how long it will be. This will allow them enough time to plan, produce and practise what is required. You will need to be specific as to what resources are available for learners to use, and how interactive you want their presentation to be.

By carrying out research, individuals are developing independent thinking and learning skills. Differentiating the task or question relevant to particular individual needs and levels will enable stretch and challenge.

Resources

- ICT equipment for creating the presentation, or pens and paper
- Computer and projector or electronic whiteboard (if relevant)
- Flip chart and pens (if relevant)
- Other resources as needed such as audio and visual aids
- Relevant items and equipment for the topic or subject

Advantages

- 👍 Supports identifying individuals who are struggling with a concept or subject
- 👍 Can be adapted to use as individual, paired work or small groups
- 👍 Supports independent research, thinking and learning skills
- 👍 Encourages teamwork (if working in groups)
- 👍 Develops presentation and communication skills and confidence
- 👍 Develops employability skills including ICT
- 👍 Can be created, completed and accessed electronically

Disadvantages

👎 Can be time-consuming to plan, assess and to provide individual feedback

👎 Can easily use up class time

👎 A time limit must be set for each presentation, which must be adhered to in order to be fair

👎 Difficult to identify who has researched what (if working in groups)

👎 Not supportive to shy learners or those lacking in confidence

👎 If set as a homework task it can be difficult to know if it is the learner's own work (an authenticity declaration could be signed by the learner)

Tip

You can plan for one or two learner presentations to be delivered over a number of sessions, rather than all the learners delivering their presentation during one session.

Further reading and weblinks

Gravells A (2017) *Principles and Practices of Teaching and Training*: Learning Matters/SAGE, London.

Skills You Need – *Top tips for effective presentations* – https://tinyurl.com/h6ea3pc

Surti J (2018) *Ultimate Presentations*: Kogan Page, London.

25 Problem sets

Individual	√	Small group	√	Large group	√
Initial	*	Formative	√	Summative	√
Informal	√	Formal	√	Preparation and marking	√
Entry Level		Level 1 and 2	√	Level 3 upwards	√

*depends upon what and how you are planning to use the approach

What is it and where can it be used?

A problem set is a challenge or a list of issues that a learner must research and find the solution to. It can be used as a teaching and learning activity or an assessment approach. The aim is for learners to familiarise themselves with the topic and then solve typical problems.

Learners should be given a set of criteria to which they will be assessed against. This could include a matrix or a grid identifying how the problem set will be assessed and scored, or a set of instructions outlining the assessment requirements.

Problem sets can be used as a group or individual approach, and completed during the session or set as a homework task. They are most commonly used in higher education but can be adapted to suit any level of learner.

If you are using problem sets as a group approach, learners must identify and agree their roles and responsibilities to ensure all group members are involved. You would also need to assess who has contributed to what.

What can it be used for?

Problem sets can be used formatively or summatively. It is a superb assessment approach which is learner centred and supports the development of problem-solving skills.

Using this approach informally will help you to identify any skills' gaps in competence, behaviours, attitudes, knowledge and/or understanding. This would enable you to give developmental advice and support to help your learners improve, e.g. learners studying GCSE Biology could be given a challenge regarding the desired characteristics of livestock, and this could be an individual or a small group problem set with different challenges, for example:

Research the advantages and disadvantages of genetic modification and selective breeding to achieve the desired characteristics for the following livestock:

- *dairy cattle which produce a higher milk yield*
- *beef cattle which produce better-quality meat*
- *sheep which produce good quality wool*

Resources

- A challenge or a list of issues to research
- Resources for learners to document their responses (paper or electronic)

Advantages

👍 Develops employability skills

👍 Develops critical thinking skills

👍 Develops communication and teambuilding skills (if used as a group activity)

Disadvantages

👎 Can be time-consuming to assess and to provide feedback to individuals

👎 Assessment can be subjective

> **Tip**
>
> If you are using this approach for summative assessment, new problem sets must be developed for each cohort of learners to prevent plagiarism.

Further reading and weblinks

The London School of Economics and Political Science – *Problem sets* – https://tinyurl.com/y6onu6hr

The Physics Classroom – *Work, energy and power: Problem set* – https://tinyurl.com/

26 Product evidence

Individual	√	Small group	√	Large group	*
Initial	√	Formative	√	Summative	√
Informal	√	Formal	√	Preparation and marking	*
Entry Level	√	Level 1 and 2	√	Level 3 upwards	√

*depends upon what and how you are planning to use the approach

What is it and where can it be used?

Product evidence is physical proof which is provided by the learner towards the requirements of a qualification or a programme of learning. It's their opportunity to prove their competence. For example, a learner studying a Level 2 Fabrication and Welding qualification would need to produce evidence of the five basic weld joints. The learner could be formatively assessed on an *Edge Joint* they have produced, and after practise, and using the feedback provided by the assessor, they can create another piece ready for summative assessment.

Assessment for product evidence could be in the workplace, a simulated working environment or within an educational setting, depending on the requirements. It could even be part of an exhibition, e.g. art or photography learners displaying their work.

What can it be used for?

There are a wide range of qualifications and programmes of learning which require product evidence, including art and design, home economics, media, engineering, information technology, cookery, and construction.

Product evidence can be used for any aspect which requires the learner to *be able to do* something or *show evidence of* something. For example, a learner being assessed for the European Computer Driving Licence (ECDL) must be able to send and receive an email; here the product evidence could be a printout or a screen shot of the emails.

Product evidence is an excellent assessment approach for vocational qualifications and it can be used informally to formatively assess and provide feedback to improve a learner's performance. It can also be used formally through summative assessment to measure a learner's competence in a particular skill.

It can also be used to assess a learner's current skills as part of the initial assessment process. By asking learners to undertake an initial assessment or skills scan (see Chapter 38), the process can identify their starting point, therefore supporting the learner to take the right qualification or programme at the correct level for them.

Resources

- A suitable environment to support the production of evidence
- The required resources needed to produce the evidence

Advantages

- Encourages independent-thinking skills
- Promotes problem-solving skills
- Allows learners to build on skills already gained
- Learners can see what they have produced
- Results can be seen immediately
- Can help to identify skills gaps

Disadvantages

- Can be expensive depending on the resources and materials used
- Can be difficult to prove it is the learner's own evidence, unless the assessor is observing at the time

---

Tip

Wherever possible, recycle or reuse physical resources to save on costs to your organisation.

Further reading and weblinks

Gravells A (2016) *Principles and Practices of Assessment*: Learning Matters/SAGE, London.

Petty G (2009) *Evidence-based Teaching: A Practical Approach* (2nd edn). Nelson Thornes, Cheltenham.

Training Qualifications UK – *The ins and outs of performance evidence* – https://tinyurl.com/yxmvjoz7

27 Professional discussion

Individual	√	Small group		Large group	
Initial		Formative	√	Summative	√
Informal	√	Formal	√	Preparation and marking	√
Entry Level	√	Level 1 and 2	√	Level 3 upwards	√

What is it and where can it be used?

A professional discussion is an in-depth, planned, two-way conversation between you and the learner about a relevant topic or subject. It is designed to assess a learner's knowledge and understanding which could also include that which underpins skills, behaviours and attitudes.

A professional discussion can be used as an assessment method in the workplace or a realistic learning environment. If it is being used formally, the discussion must be documented or recorded and cross-referenced to the assessment criteria, to enable quality assurance to take place.

What can it be used for?

A professional discussion can form evidence on a standalone basis or be part of a different assessment method, e.g. an observation (see Chapter 18). It is also a really useful assessment method to fill any evidence gaps, e.g. in assignments or practical assessments, or if you need to prove the authenticity of a learner's work.

A professional discussion can be used informally through formative assessment to measure the progress a learner is making towards a particular aspect of the topic or subject, or formally as summative assessment. Many end-point assessments for apprenticeship programmes include a professional discussion.

It is important to plan exactly what evidence is required prior to starting the professional discussion to enable you to formulate the questions and structure of the discussion. You should plan for approximately 30 to 45 minutes for the discussion and allow the learner to speak without interrupting them. It may be necessary to ask the learner further questions to build on their answers, e.g. "Can you explain why you did it that way?". Preparation is equally important, as the learner must feel at ease during the conversation to enable them to discuss or explain the aspects they are being asked about.

Resources

- A digital recording device such as a smart phone (or paper-based notes which are signed by both parties at the end of the discussion)
- Topic or subject physical resources may be required

Advantages

👍 Relatively quick to assess a learner's progress and achievements

👍 Encourages independent thinking

👍 Can challenge a learner's potential

Disadvantages

👎 Learners may become nervous, shy or anxious and not fully engage in the process

👎 Can be time-consuming to plan and prepare for

👎 Can turn into a question-and-answer session if you are not careful at managing the conversation

---

Tip

Allow the learner thinking time and do not feel you have to speak or ask more questions if there is a silence. Often learners need time to process a question before answering.

Further reading and weblinks

Black P and Wiliam D (1998) *Inside the Black Box: Raising Standards Through Classroom Assessment.* King's College School of Education, London.

Professional Assessment Ltd – Professional discussion for apprenticeship standards – https://tinyurl.com/y5yhqjh4

28 Projects

Individual	√	Small group	√	Large group	√
Initial	*	Formative	√	Summative	√
Informal	√	Formal	√	Preparation and marking	√
Entry Level	√	Level 1 and 2	√	Level 3 upwards	√

*depends upon what and how you are planning to use the approach

What is it and where can it be used?

A project is a longer-term activity which aims to meet a set of criteria or learning outcomes. It can be undertaken as part of a group or as an individual. Learners can gain knowledge and skills by working for a period of time to research and problem solve a real-life enigma, and to develop an evidence-based solution. The project should be purposeful and meaningful to help motivate the learner, and to enable them to fully engage and take ownership of their work. For example, learners studying an employability or business qualification could undertake a group project with local businesses to help them increase sustainable development. Or learners undertaking a horticultural or environmental science qualification could carry out an individual task of designing, implementing and growing a sustainable vegetable plot. Depending upon the level of learning, you could devise the project or the learners could.

Learners are continuously assessed from initial through formative to summative and no two projects are likely to be the same. Learners can develop their projects during session time, undertake directed study and work experience, work independently through homework tasks, and if working in groups through small group presentations and activities.

What can it be used for?

Project-based learning is an ideal approach to use to enable learners to achieve several criteria or learning outcomes over time. It is a great way to identify what progress learners have made in relation to their learning goals or targets. It encourages learners to problem solve, think for themselves and learn from doing; it also helps to develop reflective practice. Assessing the learner's initial plans for the project, or listening to group discussions regarding starting the project, will help you determine the level of support an individual or a group may need. It will also enable you to observe a learner's progress towards employability behaviours, skills and standards, e.g. their results focus, independence, task management, interpersonal skills, health and safety, self-awareness, ownership and responsibility, and if working in a group, their team working.

Formative assessment of the project enables you to give informal feedback regarding progress and the improvements individuals may be required to make to meet the overall criteria or learning outcomes.

Summative assessment of the project is used to confirm achievement. The feedback you give to the learner can help develop future learning and higher-level skills.

Resources

• Depends on the project undertaken

Advantages

👍 Can be interesting and motivating

👍 Can be individual or group led

👍 Allows learners to demonstrate their capabilities whilst working independently

👍 Encourages researching skills

👍 Develops problem-solving and higher-level thinking skills

Disadvantages

👎 Can be time-consuming to plan, deliver and assess, and to provide individual feedback

👎 Can easily use up class time – time limits need to be set

👎 Difficult to assess individual input (if working in groups)

👎 If set as a homework task, it can be difficult to know if it is the learner's own work (an authenticity declaration could be signed by the learner)

👎 Assessors could be biased when assessing and marking

Tip

Learners often find it easier to start their own project if you share examples of completed exemplary projects from past learners.

Further reading and weblinks

Schoology Exchange – *How students benefit for project-based assessments (with examples)* – https://tinyurl.com/y6nt9llo

SecEd – *Planning, running & assessing project-based learning in your classroom* – https://tinyurl.com/yywsl8ya

29 Questioning

Individual	√	Small group	√	Large group	*
Initial	√	Formative	√	Summative	√
Informal	√	Formal	√	Preparation and marking	√
Entry Level	√	Level 1 and 2	√	Level 3 upwards	√

depends upon what and how you are planning to use the approach

What is it and where can it be used?

Questioning is a key technique to assess knowledge and understanding, it can also stimulate a learner's thinking skills. It can be used at any time and in any context.

Examples of different types of formal and informal questioning methods are listed below (also see Chapter 20):

1. Closed questioning (*Would you ... ?*) – questions are posed to the learner which can be answered by a *yes* or *no* response. These types of responses don't demonstrate understanding.

2. Open questioning (*How would you ... ?*) – questions are posed to the learner that cannot be answered by a simple *yes* or *no*.

3. Probing questions (*Why exactly was that?*) – often used after asking an open question to encourage the learner to explore their initial answer and give more detail or information.

4. Recall and process questioning (*How did you ... ?*) – questions are set around a particular job or task which requires the learner to recall and process specific information before answering.

5. True or false – statements are read out to a group of learners and each person responds by holding up a *true* or *false* card. Only one of the responses can be correct.

What can it be used for?

Questioning can be used to assess a learner's competence, skills, behaviours, attitudes, knowledge and/or understanding. They can be used formally or informally depending on the required assessment outcome.

Questioning is a great assessment approach to identify a learner or a group of learners' starting point, e.g. a group of learners could carry out an initial assessment activity, and using the true or false questioning method, the responses would support you in identifying who has prior knowledge.

Formative assessment can be undertaken by using different questioning methods to check knowledge, skills and understanding after a topic or subject has been delivered, e.g. asking a learner to recall and explain what they have previously learned.

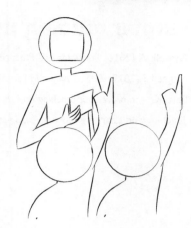

Summative assessment can utilise a range of questioning methods, but the answers will need to be documented or recorded by the assessor, or written by the learner. This is to ensure there is a record of what the learner has achieved, and for quality assurance purposes.

Resources

- Paper and pen or a device to record responses if using the activity for summative assessment
- A bank of questions
- Response cards (if using true or false responses)

Advantages

- Enables the learner to think about what they are learning
- Cost effective as resources are not usually needed
- An effective way of testing knowledge, skills and understanding
- Can be used in a wide variety of ways to suit individual needs (particularly when you are teaching groups of different levels during the same session)

Disadvantages

- Questions must be well planned to meet individual needs and enable stretch and challenge
- Questions must be unambiguous
- A shy or nervous learner might not engage well in this activity as they may struggle to answer if it's in front of their peers
- Some learners may shout out and try to answer each other's questions (if asked to the group)

> ### Tip
>
> Ensure your questions have a purpose – consider what facts or information you require as evidence towards the required outcomes.

Further reading and weblinks

Gravells A (2016) *Principles and Practices of Assessment*: Learning Matters/SAGE, London.

Mansell S (2019) *50 Teaching and Learning Approaches*: Learning Matters/SAGE, London.

Petty G – *Improve your teaching and that of your team* – https://tinyurl.com/lqusrxe

Teaching and Learning Guru – *Asking students the right questions* – https://tinyurl.com/ya7wuzvr

30 Quizzes

Individual	√	Small group	√	Large group	√
Initial	√	Formative	√	Summative	
Informal	√	Formal		Preparation and marking	*
Entry Level	√	Level 1 and 2	√	Level 3 upwards	√

*depends upon what and how you are planning to use the approach

What is it and where can it be used?

A quiz is a series of questions relating to a topic or subject which enables initial or formative assessment to take place. The quiz can be used during a session by verbally reading the questions out to the learners, who can either shout out the answers or write them down. It can be paper-based questions or be interactive using a game-based learning platform. This would allow you to devise your own online quiz; such as Kahoot!, Socrative, GoogleDocs and Plickers (see weblinks at end of chapter). Learners can answer the questions on their own devices, e.g. using their mobile phones.

Setting online quizzes as homework tasks or extension activities will enable you to send different links which have questions at different levels to your learners. This will help you to formatively assess individual progress.

What can it be used for?

Quizzes are a great assessment approach for ascertaining a learner's starting point or for measuring their progress. They can be used at any point during your session to assess learning, or at the beginning of a session to assess how much information learners have retained from a previous session. Alternatively, learners could be encouraged to create their own quiz using the assessor's parameters.

Using quizzes is an effective way to provide feedback to the learners regarding their progress, and to correct any misconceptions prior to summative assessment taking place.

Resources

- A good reliable internet connection (if an electronic or online quiz is used)
- Pens, paper or quiz sheet

- Devices with internet access for the learners to use; such as their mobile smart phones
- An interactive whiteboard (if the quiz is created electronically)

Advantages

👍 It can be engaging and fun

👍 Great for learners who are usually unwilling to participate in group work

👍 It supports social learning

👍 Measures progress

👍 A useful way to assess the retention of facts

👍 A good backup activity if you find you have spare time during a session

Disadvantages

👎 Reliance on an internet connection, and learners need a device to participate (if electronic quizzes are used)

👎 Can cause too much competitiveness

👎 Can seem trivial to some learners

👎 If you are using quizzes for learners with special educational needs and disabilities (SEND), they may require more processing time to read through the text and comprehend meaning

---

Tip

If you are using an online version of a quiz, you can add video clips and images to make it more engaging, or you can download ready-made materials and questions.

Further reading and weblinks

Bates B (2016) *A Quick Guide to Special Needs and Disabilities*: SAGE, London.

EducationQuizzes – *Why are quizzes valuable in education?* – https://tinyurl.com/y6lokzko

Google Docs – *Creating a quiz in Google Documents* – https://tinyurl.com/y8g7uqtd

Kahoot! – *What is Kahoot!?* – https://tinyurl.com/yas8lp25

Online Tools – *Plickers* – https://tinyurl.com/ya7vs2kl

Socrative – *Meet Socrative* – https://tinyurl.com/y92qk5q9

31 Recognition of prior learning (RPL)

Individual	√	Small group		Large group	
Initial	√	Formative	√	Summative	√
Informal	√	Formal	√	Preparation and marking	√
Entry Level	√	Level 1 and 2	√	Level 3 upwards	√

What is it and where can it be used?

Recognition of prior learning (RPL) is a process of identifying the knowledge and/or skills a learner has acquired throughout their lifetime, which can count towards a qualification. It can be implemented in different contexts, and evidence can be formal or informal. When using RPL as an assessment approach, the assessment requirements of a unit or qualification must be met, and recognition from the learner must be valid and reliable. Whether the evidence produced is formal or informal, learners must be able to demonstrate that they are still current with their knowledge and practice.

A learner can produce an accredited certificate as direct (formal) evidence which proves they have previously met the requirements. They could also provide indirect (informal) evidence such as personal statements, witness testimonies or supplementary evidence (skills scan, portfolio of work), which must then be assessed towards the unit and/or qualification criteria.

This assessment approach can be time-consuming and therefore costly to the organisation. A charge is often applied to the learner for undertaking the RPL process.

What can it be used for?

RPL is used to acknowledge a learner's achievement towards a unit and/or qualification, using any valid assessment approach, e.g. a professional discussion and/or examination of evidence.

The knowledge and/or skills a learner has gained can be identified and acknowledged prior to them starting their programme. For example; a learner produces direct evidence as they have achieved a Level 2 Nail Technology qualification and they are now studying Level 2 Beauty Therapy to increase their employability options. They have already achieved the mandatory *manicure and pedicure* unit and produce their certificate as evidence of achievement. A formal process of RPL then takes place by the assessor to ensure the learner does not have to repeat the same mandatory unit.

A learner could produce indirect evidence of informal on-the-job training and work experience which proves they have met certain criteria. A formal process then takes place which cross-references the learner's evidence to the assessment criteria. This can be completed by the learner but must be checked for accuracy by the assessor. This will demonstrate they already have the required knowledge and/or skills to meet the requirements. If the learner is funded through government funding, a declaration should be made to the funding organisation, as a financial deduction for the unit already achieved might be taken.

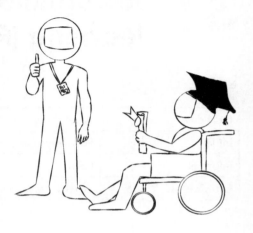

RPL can help learners to access education who have life and work experience but don't have any formal qualifications. It can also be used to assess a learner to determine the level of qualification they can work towards. For example, an adult learner who has worked a number of years in a spa as a complementary therapist would already have certain knowledge and skills. They could therefore access a level 3 or level 4 qualification directly, rather than study at level 2 before progressing to a higher level. Alternatively, a learner who has studied a related subject qualification at level 2 may access a different qualification at level 3. For example, a learner could achieve Level 2 Agriculture and then progress on to Level 3 Countryside Management rather than continue with Level 3 Agriculture.

Resources

- An organisational RPL policy
- Relevant awarding organisation guidance

Advantages

- Saves time for the learner
- Can make courses more accessible
- Validates prior learning and achievements

Disadvantages

- Time-consuming for the organisation to assess and for the learner to produce the required evidence
- The authenticity of learner evidence must be checked

Tip

Some awarding organisations have free assessment toolkits which can be accessed to support RPL decisions. It's worth finding out if this is available to you.

Further reading and weblinks

Gov.UK – *Apprenticeships: initial assessment to recognised prior learning* – https://tinyurl.com/y6db2mo3

Gravells A (2016) *Principles and Practices of Assessment*: Learning Matters/SAGE, London.

Wilson L (2012) *Practical Teaching: A Guide to Assessment and Quality Assurance*. Cengage Learning, Andover.

32 Reflective log

Individual	√	Small group	√	Large group	*
Initial		Formative	√	Summative	√
Informal	√	Formal	√	Preparation and marking	√
Entry Level		Level 1 and 2	√	Level 3 upwards	√

depends upon what and how you are planning to use the approach

What is it and where can it be used?

A reflective log, sometimes called a learning journal or diary, is a record which is produced by the learner. It is either spoken, handwritten, typed, voice recorded or videoed. It comprises of frequent entries by the learner of their experiences, thoughts and emotions about the learning process and subject they are undertaking. It can be a means of documenting ideas and personal thoughts depending on the assessment outcomes or criteria the learner is working towards.

There are two types of reflective log:

- *structured* where a learner completes a template with specific questions to support them through the process of reflection

- *unstructured* where a learner is free to record their experiences, thoughts and emotions in any format they choose

The unstructured method can be difficult to assess, as learners often move away from the assessment outcomes or criteria required.

A way for the learner to formulate their reflective log could be by using EDAR – explain, describe, analyse and revise. For example, the learner has a learning **e**xperience which can be during a session or in the workplace. They **d**escribe the experience and **a**nalyse it, e.g. what happened or why something happened in a particular way. They then **r**eflect and evaluate on how they could change or improve the experience for the future.

What can it be used for?

A reflective log can be used for practical or theoretical assessment. Learners should be encouraged to frequently record their reflections, to think more deeply about what they are writing and the experiences they have had, and to link their reflections to the criteria or assessment outcomes. Formatively assessing the reflective log and providing constructive feedback will support the learner to challenge their own behaviours and attitudes, and further improve their skills.

The benefits of a reflective log can accumulate over a period of time and are not instant. Assessment and feedback should be frequent to have any positive impact on the learner.

Resources

- Depends upon what and how you are planning to use the approach

Advantages

👍 Helps you to develop a better understanding of individual learners

👍 Improves written work (if using a written reflective method)

👍 Supports critical thinking skills

👍 Can be motivational

👍 Builds on current knowledge, skills and understanding

👍 Useful for self-assessment

Disadvantages

👎 Can be time-consuming to assess and provide feedback

👎 Usually undertaken over a longer period of time

👎 Some learners may not be completely honest or think they have achieved more (or less) than they actually have

👎 Confidentiality must be adhered to

👎 Some learners might not complete their reflective logs on a regular basis (or might write them at the last minute), and therefore without ongoing feedback, it might not have a positive impact on their learning

---

Tip

A reflective log template with subheadings will support new learners to better engage in the process of reflective learning.

Further reading and weblinks

Gravells A (2016) *Principles and Practice of Assessment*: Learning Matters/SAGE, London.

Gravells A (2017) *Principles and Practices of Teaching and Training*: Learning Matters/SAGE London.

Read H (2016) *The Best Assessor's Guide*: Read On Publications Ltd, Bideford.

33 Report writing

Individual	√	Small group	√	Large group	√
Initial		Formative	√	Summative	√
Informal		Formal	√	Preparation and marking	√
Entry Level		Level 1 and 2	√	Level 3 upwards	√

What is it and where can it be used?

Report writing is about giving learners a scenario, question or topic to research. Once they have completed the research activity they must write a formal report.

Report writing is different from essay writing (see Chapter 9) as it focuses on facts rather than arguments or reasoning. It is written for a particular purpose and audience; it should be concise and make recommendations. For example, learners studying a Waste Management degree are asked to research household recycling and the impact on the environment. They must write a report detailing their findings and recommendations in 3000 words, with a 10% allowance either way, for submission to a hypothetical local town council.

Report writing should have a maximum word count. It must follow a format, e.g. an introduction or overview of the research undertaken, followed by the findings, a summary of the major points, any recommendations and a conclusion. It should be written in the third person and supported throughout with academic references which relate to the research activity. Referencing is usually a requirement for level 3 and above. Further information regarding referencing can be found in the links at the end of the chapter.

The learner has a set time frame, usually a period of a few weeks, to complete the research activity. It should be set as a homework task, be self-study, can be completed in session time or in combination. You will need to ensure that each learner signs a declaration stating the work is their own.

What can it be used for?

Report writing is ideal for higher-level learners to enable them to demonstrate their knowledge and understanding of a topic or subject.

Report writing can help to develop learners' research and communication skills. It also supports the development of different writing styles as they must write the report for a particular audience.

Resources

- A relevant research question or topic
- Electronic device such as a word processor or pens and paper

Advantages

👍 Encourages analytical and critical thinking skills

👍 Develops employability skills

👍 Useful for academic and theoretical subjects

👍 Supports the development of literacy and language skills

Disadvantages

👎 Can be time-consuming to mark, assess and provide individual feedback

👎 Can be subjective between different assessors when marking

👎 Plagiarism can be an issue

Tip

At first, learners may struggle with the concept of report writing. It is beneficial to provide them with subheadings to help them format their report.

Further reading and weblinks

Academic skills – http://libguides.staffs.ac.uk/refzone/harvard/

Harvard Generator referencing – https://tinyurl.com/3684hax

SkillsYOUNEED – *How to write a report* – https://tinyurl.com/ybc635ek

University of Leicester – *Writing reports* – https://tinyurl.com/y22gxoz7

34 Role play

Individual	√	Small group	√	Large group	√
Initial	√	Formative	√	Summative	
Informal	√	Formal		Preparation and marking	√
Entry Level	√	Level 1 and 2	√	Level 3 upwards	√

What is it and where can it be used?

Role play is a technique which allows learners to be informally assessed in different situations. This enables them to demonstrate how they would deal with a situation that they may encounter in real life, in a realistic but supportive setting. It enables learners to develop skills and strategies which will help them in the future, by assuming the role of another person or acting out a scenario. For example; if you wish your learners to role play how to manage an angry customer, the activity could take ten minutes followed by a discussion and feedback. If your learners are developing skills such as assuming the role of a salon manager in a realistic hairdressing working environment, it could take two to three hours.

Depending upon the size of your group, you could have smaller groups working together on the same or different situations. Learners could then demonstrate their role play in front of their peers.

Role play can be used in the classroom or a workshop to act out a situation or scenario, or in a realistic working environment, e.g. to develop employability skills. It can help put theory into practice, however clear roles and time limits will need to be defined beforehand.

What can it be used for?

Role play can be used to formatively assess a learner's progress towards developing communication, problem solving and/or employability skills. It enables the learner to demonstrate their current skills, knowledge and understanding. You can see whether they have made progress from their starting point, and how they react in different situations.

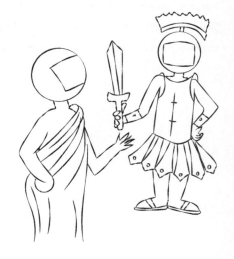

Pairs or small groups of learners could act out a scenario and be observed by their peers (see Chapter 21), who could then ask questions and/or give feedback. This would help develop observation, questioning and communication skills.

Resources

- A realistic working environment if you are assessing skills for employment
- A classroom or workshop if you are assessing communication and problem-solving skills

Advantages

👍 Enables hands-on practice to apply new skills in a safe and realistic setting

👍 Allows decision making and problem solving

👍 Develops understanding from a different perspective

👍 Demonstrates the current skills level

👍 Links theory to practice

Disadvantages

👎 Can be difficult to engage learners who are easily embarrassed or lack confidence

👎 Can quickly become disorganised if not kept under control

👎 Difficult to keep all learners engaged at the same time

👎 Not all learners will take it seriously or may overact

Tip

Ensure all learners fully understand their role, and the purpose of the activity and assessment process, prior to commencing.

Further reading and weblinks

British Council – *Role-play* – https://tinyurl.com/yytor9k3

Gravells A (2017) *Principles and Practices of Teaching and Training*: Learning Matters/SAGE, London.

Mansell S (2019) *50 Teaching and Learning Approaches*: Learning Matters/SAGE, London.

35 Self-assessment

Individual	√	Small group	√	Large group	√
Initial	√	Formative	√	Summative	√
Informal	√	Formal	√	Preparation and marking	√
Entry Level	√	Level 1 and 2	√	Level 3 upwards	√

What is it and where can it be used?

Self-assessment is an excellent assessment approach to enable learners to identify gaps in their own competence, skills, behaviours, attitudes, knowledge and/or understanding. It helps develops learners' self-awareness and supports them to take responsibility for their own learning. When embedded as part of a programme of learning it can enable rapid progress.

Self-assessment takes place when a learner reflects and evaluates their own work or performance. It can be used during a session, in the workplace, or set as a homework task.

Examples could include a learner:

- awarding themself a grade for a presentation they have delivered
- suggesting improvements regarding their skills and knowledge
- compiling a learner statement (see Chapter 14) of what they have achieved regarding certain assessment criteria.

What can it be used for?

Self-assessment can be an individual or a group task. It can also be used as a learning activity as well as an assessment approach. It can be used for initial, formative or summative assessment, and can be formal or informal. For example:

- Initial assessment – learners could complete a *personal skill review* identifying what they think they are good at and what they think they need to improve. This could be written in an essay format (see Chapter 9) or a reflective log (see Chapter 32). Alternatively, learners could grade themselves on a sliding scale of *one to five* for personal skills such as communication skills, planning and organisational skills, personal confidence and independence. This could be revisited every few weeks to measure progress.
- Formative assessment – asking learners to identify what they did well and what they did least well, or found difficult. This will help to determine how they are progressing and what they need to do to improve or develop further.
- Summative assessment – a reflective log (see Chapter 32) could be written by the learner which details their strengths, weaknesses and areas that require improvement.

However, it is difficult to validate what's been written as you only have the learner's word for it. The assessor must be able to judge that the learner's work is theirs, if it is going to be used as part of a final assessment.

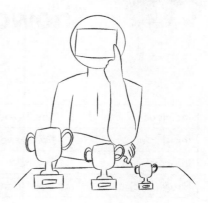

Using self-assessment as an informal formative assessment approach will support learners to develop employability skills as well as preparing them for long-term employment. However, learners do need to understand what they are self-assessing towards, and be honest, specific and concise with their responses.

Resources

- Depends on how you are using the approach

Advantages

- 👍 Encourages independence
- 👍 Promotes learners' involvement
- 👍 Develops critical-thinking skills
- 👍 Develops employability skills

Disadvantages

- 👎 Can be inaccurate as learners might feel they have achieved more (or less) than they actually have
- 👎 Not all learners will engage in the process
- 👎 Difficult to authenticate

Tip

Combining peer assessment (see Chapter 21) alongside self-assessment could save you valuable assessment time. Discussing their self-assessment decisions with a peer will help to support learners to develop accurate self-assessment skills.

Further reading and weblinks

Gravells A (2016) *Principles and Practices of Assessment*: Learning Matters/SAGE: London.

Peer and self-assessment – https://tinyurl.com/yy64vbsk

Petty, G – *Self assessment* – https://tinyurl.com/yygsgx7y

UNSW Sydney – *Student self-assessment* – https://tinyurl.com/y6dzvygg

36 Showcase

Individual	√	Small group		Large group	
Initial		Formative	√	Summative	√
Informal		Formal	√	Preparation and marking	√
Entry Level		Level 1 and 2	√	Level 3 upwards	√

What is it and where can it be used?

Showcase is a formal assessment approach which requires the learner to present their work to an assessor or a panel of experts.

During their programme, learners build a portfolio of evidence which could include work-based evidence, research activities, the results of tests and exams, work-based documentation, projects and assignments. These demonstrate their competence, skills, behaviours, attitudes, knowledge and/or understanding towards a particular topic, subject or job role. The learner must showcase their portfolio of evidence to an assessor or a panel of experts through a formal presentation. This demonstrates what they have done to achieve the required learning outcomes or standards.

Showcase is often used as part of the end-point assessment process for apprenticeship programmes, and is broken down into different tasks. For example, a learner undertaking the Level 2 Customer Service Practitioner Standard must complete three tasks for the showcase assessment section. Tasks 1 and 2 can be evidenced in a variety of ways but Task 3 must be work-based. The learner will showcase their work to someone they have never met before, therefore they will need to prepare well.

What can it be used for?

Showcase is a fantastic summative assessment approach as it enables learners to demonstrate what they know and can do. By presenting their evidence to an assessor or a panel of experts, learners are demonstrating how they have applied and used the required competence, skills, behaviours, attitudes, knowledge and/or understanding to meet the learning outcomes or standards over an agreed period of time.

Showcase can also be used as a formative assessment approach to check a learner's knowledge and understanding at a given point in time, and to measure their progress towards achieving a formal qualification.

Resources

- Depends on how the approach is used

Advantages

- 👍 Helps the learners to develop confidence and improve their communication skills
- 👍 Promotes independence and creativity
- 👍 Promotes organisational skills
- 👍 It's interactive and learner centred
- 👍 Helps to develop problem-solving and independent-thinking skills

Disadvantages

- 👎 A time limit must be agreed and adhered to, otherwise the learner might over-run or digress
- 👎 Can be subjective between assessors or panels of experts
- 👎 Learners may become anxious and not present to the best of their ability

---

Tip

Sometimes, learners can become anxious about presenting their showcase. A great way to prepare learners for the summative assessment is to allow them to informally present their showcase to each other beforehand.

Further reading and weblinks

Authentic Assessment Toolbox – *Portfolios* – https://tinyurl.com/7n5m7wa

Education & Training Foundation – *Online support for end-point assessment* – https://tinyurl.com/y67k5eys

The Strategic Development Network – *The Presentation/Showcase – Under the bonnet of end-point assessment* – https://tinyurl.com/yxqeh9gj

37 Simulation

Individual	√	Small group	√	Large group	*
Initial	√	Formative	√	Summative	√
Informal	√	Formal	√	Preparation and marking	*
Entry Level	√	Level 1 and 2	√	Level 3 upwards	√

*depends upon what and how you are planning to use the approach

What is it and where can it be used?

Simulation is an imitation activity, carried out when the real activity would be too dangerous or difficult for the learner to undertake. The simulation allows learners to demons-trate and be assessed safely, as if they were in a real situation. For the simulation to work it is vital that the activity being assessed reflects real practice and genuine situations.

The simulated assessment could be a practical activity, e.g. cutting hair using a wig, or a computer-generated activity, e.g. making corporate decisions as an assigned virtual character.

The simulation should be planned well in advance and the activity set at a level which meets individual needs. This will naturally allow each individual to be stretched and challenged at the appropriate pace and level.

What can it be used for?

Simulation is usually used to prepare learners for employment and is ideal practice, prior to them being in a real working environment. Undertaking formal or informal formative assessment to measure learners' progress, and providing feedback after the simulation, will support them to improve their performance, prior to summative assessment taking place.

For example; a forensic science learner could be observed in a simulated crime scene. They will be able to demonstrate that they can carry out fingerprint analysis, DNA analysis, and collect samples and materials relating to the simulated crime.

Simulation can also be used as part of the initial assessment process to enable you to ascertain a learner's starting point, prior to enrolling them onto a programme of study.

Resources

* Specialist equipment and materials (depending on the simulation)

Advantages

👍 Helps learners to develop confidence in a safe environment

👍 Interactive and learner centred

👍 Helps to develop problem-solving and independent-thinking skills

Disadvantages

👎 Careful planning is needed

👎 Can be time-consuming

👎 Specialist equipment may be needed

👎 Not all learners will take the assessment seriously

👎 Learners might act completely differently in a real situation

---

Tip

If the learning programme is accredited, you will need to check with the awarding organisation if simulated evidence is acceptable.

Further reading and weblinks

Ellington et al. (1998) *Using Games and Simulations in the Classroom*: Kogan Page, London.

Jones K (1995) *Simulations: A Handbook for Teachers and Trainers*: Kogan Page. London.

Rawlings et al. (2014) *Using Simulation in Assessment and Teaching*: CSWE Press, Washington, DC.

Teaching with simulations – https://serc.carleton.edu/sp/library/simulations/index.html

38 Skills scan

Individual	√	Small group	√	Large group	√
Initial	√	Formative	√	Summative	
Informal	√	Formal	√	Preparation and marking	√
Entry Level	√	Level 1 and 2	√	Level 3 upwards	√

What is it and where can it be used?

A skills scan is a test which determines the level, skill, experience, or previous knowledge for a particular topic or subject a learner may have. The scan (or test) is created by the assessor and can be written, online, computer based, or a practical task. It is usually undertaken before or at the start of a learning programme as part of the initial assessment process. The results will help to determine the most appropriate course and level a learner should be able to access. For example, a learner wanting to study Swedish Massage who already holds a Level 3 Complementary Therapies' qualification could be asked to demonstrate a massage technique to show the skills they have already achieved.

What can it be used for?

Skills scans are a brilliant assessment approach to determine a learner's starting point. They can be used to gather a wide range of information about a learner prior to them starting a programme. They can also be used for individual target setting to support the learner to progress through their programme. For example, a learner could be tested to determine their level of maths and English: this would be known as an initial assessment. They could then be tested further on their areas of strength and areas of weakness. This would be known as a diagnostic assessment.

From the information gathered, a unique, sequenced and individualised programme can be agreed with the learner to improve their maths and English. Progress measures can be made by testing the learner either with a formal exam or by them repeating the initial assessment to see if they have progressed to a higher level.

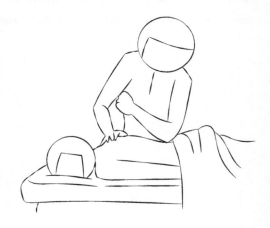

A skills scan can also be used to test a learner's practical ability. For example, a learner may have self-assessed themselves as an advanced horse rider. A skills scan could be undertaken on a horse suitable for novices, and in a safe environment, to determine if the learner was indeed an advanced rider or a novice rider. Using the skills scan results would ensure the learner was matched to the correct horse and ability, to improve their horse-riding skills.

Skills scans are also a useful assessment approach to use prior to starting a new topic or subject, as it helps determine what a learner already knows and can do. This will enable you to tailor the delivery of the topic or subject to suit the individual learner, enabling rapid progress.

Resources

- Depends on how you are using the approach

Advantages

- Enables objective and effective comparisons (for online and computer-based assessment)
- Helps to determine a learner's starting point to enable tailor-made delivery
- Can support learners to progress rapidly

Disadvantages

- Can be subjective (for a practical assessment of ability)
- Learner may get nervous and not perform as well as usual
- Feedback from the results of computer and online tests might not be useful or developmental

---

Tip

It is important to record or document all the evidence produced from a skills scan, to determine the measure of progress at a later date.

Further reading and weblinks

Gravells A (2016) *Principles and Practices of Assessment*: Learning Matters/SAGE, London.

Wallace S (2005) *Teaching and Supporting Learning in Further Education* (2nd edn): Learning Matters, Exeter.

39 Three, two, one

Individual	√	Small group	√	Large group	√
Initial		Formative	√	Summative	
Informal	√	Formal		Preparation and marking	√
Entry Level	√	Level 1 and 2	√	Level 3 upwards	√

What is it and where can it be used?

Three, two, one is an informal assessment approach which helps you to measure learners' progress. It can identify any areas where they may be having difficulty understanding, and therefore need further support with.

After delivering a topic or subject, you could ask your learners to complete the three, two, one activity by writing a response to each of the following:

Three – Write three key facts you have learnt during today's session

Two – Write two questions for something you need further clarity on

One – Write one thing you found interesting and would like to learn more about

This assessment approach should be completed after the delivery of a topic or subject and it can follow a practical or a theoretical session.

What can it be used for?

Three, two, one is a quick and easy formative assessment approach which supports you to assess the progress learners are making towards a particular topic or subject.

The responses you receive from the learners will help you identify any adjustments that need to be made to your delivery. For example, if most of the learners have identified the same two questions, or if they have answered the three key facts incorrectly. You can then adjust your delivery to address the gaps. If it's a large group of learners, they could discuss their responses amongst themselves in small groups first. They could then summarise the points, with one person from each group reading these out.

Three, two, one can also be used as a teaching and learning approach to recap a topic or subject.

Resources

- Paper and pens, or electronic devices to make notes

Advantages

 Helps to develop independent thinking and learning skills

Is learner centred

Helps learners to enhance their knowledge of any topic and also evaluate information

Quick and easy to use

Disadvantages

Not all learners may want to take part

Requires learners to be self-motivated

Tip

This assessment approach can be adapted for lower-level learners by allowing them to respond verbally.

Further reading and weblinks

Facing History and Ourselves – *3-2-1* – https://tinyurl.com/y3szt3r5

Mansell S (2019) *50 Teaching and Learning Approaches*: Learning Matters/SAGE, London.

Theteacherstoolkit – *3-2-1* – https://tinyurl.com/og5lo79

40 Tutorial review

Individual	√	Small group		Large group	
Initial	*	Formative	√	Summative	
Informal	√	Formal	√	Preparation and marking	√
Entry Level	√	Level 1 and 2	√	Level 3 upwards	√

depends upon what and how you are planning to use the approach

What is it and where can it be used?

A tutorial review is a one-to-one discussion between the assessor and the learner. The focus of the discussion is on the development of a learner's competence, skills, behaviours, attitudes, knowledge and/or understanding. The first tutorial review is used to talk about and identify the learner's starting point. This can be based on using initial assessment information and the learner's intended career or personal goal. The learner and assessor will agree short-term *SMART* (**s**pecific, **m**easurable, **a**chievable, **r**elevant and **t**imebound) targets to support the learner in progressing towards their ultimate goal.

Subsequent tutorial reviews should focus on the progress made regarding the previously set targets. If the targets are assessed as achieved, new *SMART* targets can be agreed and set. If the targets have not been achieved, a discussion should be held to identify the reasons why. If there are any barriers to learning which require support, the targets can be modified to make them achievable for the learner, or the dates can be amended.

The tutorial reviews should be held every eight to twelve weeks (or according to your organisation's requirements) and in a quiet area if possible. The number of discussions will depend on the length of the programme and the individual learner's needs. It can be held face to face, using a range of media, or via the telephone or online. A copy of the record of the tutorial review should be given to the learner to enable them to revisit their targets, or be accessible electronically.

What can it be used for?

Tutorial reviews are formative and form a very important aspect of the learner journey. They can enable learners to identify their own progress throughout the duration of their programme. They also give learners an opportunity to discuss any issues or difficulties they may be experiencing with the programme, or any additional support needs which had not been identified at the beginning of the programme.

Some targets could be linked directly to the learning programme, e.g. a learner studying Level 3 Team Leading could be given a target of presenting a project to their peers in preparation for their end-point assessment. However, targets should not be driven solely by competence, skills, knowledge and/or under-standing towards the learning programme. They should also be linked to improving a learner's softer transferable skills such as behaviours and attitudes, e.g.: developing confidence, time keeping, communication, teamwork, problem solving, and planning and organising skills. In addition, targets should be set in relation to improving an individual's applied maths and English skills, e.g. calcu-lating VAT for maths, or improving spelling, grammar and/or punctuation through written assignments for English.

Resources

- A means of documenting or recording the tutorial review (paper or electronic)

Advantages

👍 Can help improve academic and vocational performance

👍 Encourages self-directed learning

👍 Enables targeted support which can lead to rapid progress

Disadvantages

👎 Records must be maintained (a mandatory requirement for funded programmes)

👎 Can be time-consuming to carry out

Tip

Formalise the process by timetabling tutorial review sessions; this will enable learners to prepare for the discussion. If this is during class time, other learners in the group should continue working whilst you carry out the individual reviews.

Further reading and weblinks

Gravells A (2016) *Principles and Practices of Assessment*: Learning Matters/SAGE, London.

Petty G (2014) *Teaching Today*: Oxford University Press, Oxford.

41 Two-stage digest

Individual	√	Small group	√	Large group			√
Initial		Formative	√	Summative			√
Informal	√	Formal	√	Preparation and marking			√
Entry Level		Level 1 and 2	√	Level 3 upwards			√

What is it and where can it be used?

Two-stage digest is an assessment approach to measure knowledge and understanding. It can be completed during a session or set as a homework task; alternatively, it can be a combination of both.

For the first stage, learners are given a question, statement or topic to research and are asked to write an essay detailing their findings (see Chapter 9). They are given a maximum word count of 1000 words and a minimum word count of 800 words. The essays are then assessed and handed back to the learners with developmental feedback.

The second stage requires learners to make any amendments to the essay and then summarise the key points in a maximum of 100 words or 200 characters.

What can it be used for?

Two-stage digest can be used as a formal or informal assessment approach. The first stage can be used for summative assessment. The second stage is a useful assessment approach to check the learners' knowledge and understanding of the research they have undertaken. By having to condense their writing into so few words or characters to identify the key points of their research, learners need to understand what they have written.

The second stage could be reduced by using bullet points, or learners could be asked to write the summary for a social media post, e.g. Twitter which allows a maximum of 280 characters per Tweet, a Facebook page description which allows 155 characters, Snapchat which allows up to 80 characters, or any other relevant social media. Learners don't have to use social media (if it's not relevant at the time), as they can use a word processor or hand-write their work, but the nature of the activity will help them to focus.

Resources

- A research question, statement or topic
- Electronic device such as a word processor, or pens and paper
- A method of counting words or characters (if hand-written)
- Access to a device which is internet enabled (if using social media)

Advantages

- Can be used for formative and summative assessment
- Checks learners' knowledge and understanding
- Encourages creative-thinking and problem-solving skills
- Useful for academic and theoretical subjects
- Supports the development of literacy and language skills

Disadvantages

- Can be time-consuming to assess and provide individual feedback
- Can be subjective when marking
- Plagiarism can be an issue

Tip

If your organisation has a learning platform which learners can access, rather than use social media, you could set up a page for learners to post their work to. Alternatively, a closed or private social media group could be created for learners to communicate and share ideas.

Further reading and weblinks

London College of International Business Studies – *The role of social media in education* – https://tinyurl.com/yyfwt8rl

Manchester Metropolitan University – *Creative teaching* – https://tinyurl.com/y4w875tg

University of Leicester – *Social media in teaching and learning* – https://tinyurl.com/y2yfou3q

42 Venn diagram

Individual	√	Small group	√	Large group	
Initial	*	Formative	√	Summative	√
Informal	√	Formal	√	Preparation and marking	√
Entry Level	√	Level 1 and 2	√	Level 3 upwards	√

depends upon what and how you are planning to use the approach

What is it and where can it be used?

A Venn diagram is an illustration of the relationship between and among groups of objects or phenomena that share something in common. The illustration is made up of overlapping circles, usually two or three, to represent a visual method to compare and contrast information. It is most commonly used in mathematical and scientific subjects such as engineering or computer science, but it can be adapted for almost any subject and level. The following process should be used:

1. Learners are given the titles of two or three objects or phenomena that have similarities and differences (i.e. to compare and contrast)

2. Learners are then given a Venn diagram template or are asked to draw two or three circles which overlap in the middle

3. Learners identify the differences and write these in the outer section/s of the circle

4. Learners identify the similarities and write these in the overlapping section/s of the circles

For example, comparing and contrasting apples and oranges. Learners could draw two circles slightly overlapping each other; each circle represents one of the fruits and should be labelled as an apple or orange. Learners write down information about each of the fruits, and if there is a comparison, such as both are a fruit, both have pips and both grow on trees, they write these in the overlapping section of the circles. Any contrasts should be written in the outer section of the circle such as colour, texture and edible parts.

This is called a Venn diagram as it was invented by John Venn (1834–1923).

What can it be used for?

Venn diagrams can be used formally or informally and are an effective assessment approach to measure knowledge and understanding and to check memory recall.

It's an ideal activity to use at the end of a module or unit as a summative assessment. Alternatively, it can be used as a formative assessment at the start of a session as a recap from the previous session. Learners will visually represent the information that they remember.

Venn diagrams can also be used for initial assessment, e.g. a learner choosing to studying physics could be asked to compare and contrast different types of volcanoes.

Resources

- Paper or a template and coloured pens, or suitable electronic devices
- Something to draw a circle with such as a compass (if drawing by hand)

Advantages

👍 Encourages learners to discover new information by building on what they already know

👍 Supports learners to communicate ideas and thoughts

👍 Helps learners to enhance knowledge of any topic, and to evaluate information

Disadvantages

👎 Marking and assessment can be time-consuming

👎 Less visual or less creative learners may struggle to engage with the activity

---

Tip

Asking learners to use coloured pens can encourage creativity. Alternatively, Venn diagrams could be created digitally, e.g. by using a computer or a suitable electronic device.

Further reading and weblinks

ARBs – *Venn diagrams* – https://tinyurl.com/yxtw67ah

John Venn – www.biography.com/scientist/john-venn

Owlcation – *Venn Diagram: An overview of an effective learning tool* – https://tinyurl.com/y2zwhwww

Top Notch Teaching – *3 easy ways to make teaching Venn diagrams fun* – https://tinyurl.com/y54u65lud

43 Video

Individual	√	Small group	√	Large group	
Initial	√	Formative	√	Summative	√
Informal	√	Formal	√	Preparation and marking	√
Entry Level	√	Level 1 and 2	√	Level 3 upwards	√

What is it and where can it be used?

A video is a visual media source with audio which records moving pictures and sound. It is a wide-ranging assessment approach which can be used formally or informally to enable learners to demonstrate what they can do. It can be used anywhere the learner has access to the required tools, equipment and materials. Learners might need permission from those who will be included, i.e. that they are happy to be recorded. In addition, learners must agree to follow any confidentiality requirements, e.g. if they are working in a care home or with children.

Learners will need to be given clear criteria of what is required for the assessment process, including the content and length of the video. It can be recorded on any digital mobile device which has a camera and recording facility such as an android phone or a digital video camera. Learners can set the camera up and leave it running, or they could ask a peer or a colleague to record them. It is also useful to have access to a tripod to keep the camera steady. A microphone might be required if a mobile device is used which does not pick up sound from a distance.

What can it be used for?

Video is a great assessment approach for summative assessment. For example, learners studying Level 3 Horticulture are required to prepare and establish propagation material. Evidence of seed propagation could be videoed by placing the camera on or near to the propagation station to video the learner demonstrating and explaining the task.

To check learners' knowledge and understanding, video can be used formatively. For example, a small group of learners could be given different research activities and asked to create a video to present back to their peers.

This would enable the assessor to establish the progress the learners have made, correct any misconceptions, and allow peer assessment to take place.

Video can also be used for initial assessment. For example, a learner could be given a set of questions asking them to explain or demonstrate their current knowledge and skills, by recording their verbal responses or showing their evidence.

Depending upon how the video evidence will be assessed, it might be necessary to ask further questions of the learner, to clarify any points not demonstrated.

Resources

- Technical equipment to record the video
- Data storage and/or a way of saving the video
- Technical equipment or apps to play the video
- Editing equipment or apps (if necessary)
- Tools, equipment and materials relating to the task

Advantages

- Is direct proof of what a learner has achieved, i.e. is authentic
- Can be assessed and quality assured after the event
- Can be fun and engaging

Disadvantages

- Relies on learners and assessors having access to technical equipment
- Can be expensive to set up if the equipment is not normally available
- Technical support may be required
- Learners may not take it seriously

Tip

Explain to your learners that they may need approval to record a video in some places, along with gaining the permission of those involved. This might need to be written rather than verbally stated.

Further reading and weblinks

EdSurge – *Video assignments are the new term paper: How does that change teaching and learning?* – https://tinyurl.com/y3qmd7eg

Teachthought – *How I use video for assessment in my classroom* – https://tinyurl.com/y4duvgy6

44 Viva

Individual	√	Small group		Large group	
Initial		Formative	√	Summative	√
Informal		Formal	√	Preparation and marking	√
Entry Level		Level 1 and 2		Level 3 upwards	√

What is it and where can it be used?

A viva is a spoken exam often used in higher education as an approach towards assessing academic qualifications. Learners are asked specific questions by an assessor or a panel of assessors in relation to their personal statements or another piece of submitted written work. The assessors might be referred to as *examiners*. If the work is being assessed by a panel, this often includes industry representatives as well as academics to make up the group of experts.

The viva can last for between 30 and 90 minutes depending on the awarding organisation's requirements, and it is usually held in a classroom or meeting room.

Some end-point assessment standards use an approach very similar to a viva (see Chapter 8).

What can it be used for?

The viva enables the learner to demonstrate that the work is their own by confirming their understanding of what they have written. The assessor will ask questions in relation to the strengths and weaknesses of the submitted work, giving the learner the opportunity to demonstrate their aptitude and critical thinking skills.

Questions generally used in a viva are:

- What is your work about?
- Why did you choose …?
- How did you find out …?
- What did you find?
- Were you surprised at any of your findings?
- Why does it matter?
- What else could you have done?

Once the viva is complete, the assessor will accumulate the result (usually pass or fail) and recommend the learner's next steps. Depending on the awarding organisation's requirements, there may be an option to refer the learner and enable them to resubmit.

Resources

- A suitable quiet environment

Advantages

👍 Assesses communication skills

👍 Authenticates the learner's knowledge and understanding

👍 Provides flexibility to discuss weak areas

Disadvantages

👎 Lacks standardisation and can permit favouritism

👎 Time-consuming to carry out with each learner

👎 Can be stressful for the learner

Tip

Carrying out a practice mini viva with your learners will help them prepare for their actual viva.

Further reading and weblinks

S.T.A.R.S – *Oral examinations for undergraduate students – (the 'viva')* – https://tinyurl.com/y3usu75u

The Guardian – *How to survive a PhD viva: 17 top tips* – https://tinyurl.com/ybmlz9ke

University of Leicester – *Preparing for your viva* – https://tinyurl.com/y6y7qcrm

45 Vlogs, blogs and podcasts

Individual	√	Small group	√	Large group	
Initial	√	Formative	√	Summative	√
Informal	√	Formal	√	Preparation and marking	√
Entry Level	√	Level 1 and 2	√	Level 3 upwards	√

What is it and where can it be used?

Vlogs, blogs, and podcasts are assessment approaches where learners use technology to document their learning by:

- filming
- writing
- recording

A vlog is a short video clip which is approximately seven minutes in length. It is filmed by the learner and details the learning activities they have undertaken. It can combine text, sound and images. Each clip is recorded over a period of time.

A blog is a log of learning activities written by the learner; it is usually between 1000 and 2000 words. It often takes the form of a diary with relevant information in chronological order.

A podcast is a succinct recording (usually between 10 to 45 minutes) of a learner's voice explaining the learning activities they have undertaken. Podcasts can also have video attached to them.

All three approaches require learners to frequently film, document or record the activities they have undertaken. They then post these online or to a learning platform on a regular basis.

You should give your learners instructions with clear criteria of what is required for the activity. For example, you could ask learners to keep a learning log of their activities for a particular topic or subject by using a vlog, a blog or a podcast twice a week over a period of six weeks. Learners could be given a set word count or time limit for each log, depending on the approach you are using.

Vlogs, blogs, and podcasts can be used in the classroom or set as a homework task. They can be used anywhere that the learner has access to the required technology and data storage. Note that vlogs tend to require more data storage than blogs or podcasts.

They could be used by small groups to work collaboratively on a topic and be conversational rather than purely factual. An online blog used by more than one person is known as a Wiki, e.g. Wikipedia is an online encyclopaedia which many people can contribute towards.

What can it be used for?

Vlogs, blogs, and podcasts are all brilliant formative assessment approaches which can be used for individual or group activities. For example, they are an ideal approach for an individual to use as an unstructured reflective log (see Chapter 32), or a small group of learners could be asked to review products related to the subject they are studying to demonstrate their knowledge and understanding. An individual learner or groups of learners could be asked to demonstrate their learning of a concept, topic or subject by creating a series of vlogs, blogs or podcasts.

Peer assessment (see Chapter 21) could also be included in formative assessment by encouraging learners to share their work with each other.

All three approaches can also be used as supplementary evidence towards summative assessment, e.g. to support an essay, observation, interview, or to be included as part of a presentation.

Resources

- Technical and electronic equipment, and/or relevant software and apps to create and play the vlogs, blogs and podcasts
- Data storage
- Editing equipment or apps
- Tools, equipment and materials relating to the task

Advantages

- It is direct proof of what a learner has achieved
- Can be assessed after the event
- Can be fun and engaging

Disadvantages

- Relies on learners and assessors having access to technical equipment, and knowing how to use it
- Technical support may be required
- Learners may not take it seriously

> ### Tip
>
> Encourage your learners to research the assessment approach before trying it out, e.g. learners who are going to use a vlog could watch examples on YouTube.

Further reading and weblinks

Atherton P (2018) *50 Ways to use technology enhanced learning in the classroom*: Learning Matters/SAGE, London.

educationcloset – *Podcasting in the classroom* – https://tinyurl.com/y3avubzu

eLearning Industry – *How to use Wiki in the classroom* – https://tinyurl.com/y44mbfmn

Scott D (2018) *Learning Technology: A Handbook for FE Teachers and Assessors*: Critical Publishing Ltd, St Albans.

Social Media and the classroom – *BLOG* –- https://tinyurl.com/y6lkmag6

Social Media and the classroom – *VLOG* – https://tinyurl.com/y64njds8

46 Walk and talk

Individual	√	Small group		Large group	
Initial		Formative	√	Summative	√
Informal	√	Formal	√	Preparation and marking	√
Entry Level	√	Level 1 and 2	√	Level 3 upwards	√

What is it and where can it be used?

Walk and talk is a hands-on assessment activity which is carried out with a learner during a session or in the workplace. It is usually associated with a workplace routine or job, where the learner *walks and talks* the assessor through a process.

The learner is required to demonstrate their competence, skills, behaviours, attitudes, knowledge and/or understanding of a particular task relating to the assessment criteria. They do this by showing and explaining to you, how they would undertake the task. For example, a learner studying the level 2 Customer Service Practitioner Standards must *deal with customer conflict and challenge*. By giving the learner different scenarios as formative assessment, they could talk you through the processes they would use to manage the customer. This would include how they could resolve any issues to best meet the customer's needs and manage their expectations. The learner would show you any documentation they would be required to complete, and explain the level of detail they would include in the documentation.

What can it be used for?

It can be used for formative assessment to measure a learner's progress towards an outcome, or summative assessment to confirm competence, skills, behaviours, attitudes, knowledge and/or understanding.

As a formative assessment activity, walk and talk is a fantastic tool to build a learner's confidence in what could be a difficult workplace task. It enables you to identify what the learner is doing well and where they need further development. For example, a learner studying a Level 2 Certificate in Animal Care must demonstrate their knowledge and skills in preparing feed for animals. The learner would start by washing their hands and explaining the reason and importance of personal hygiene. They would

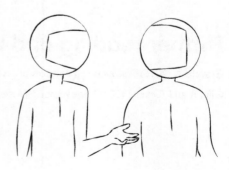

identify and prepare the feed, describing the correct equipment and utensils, and explain why they had selected and prepared the feed in a particular way. They would also discuss any precautions that should be taken when preparing the feed, including any health and safety legislation.

If you are using walk and talk as a summative assessment activity, you will need to check the assessment criteria and range, to ensure the awarding organisation will accept the evidence.

Resources

- Paper and pen or an electronic device to document or record the learner undertaking the task
- A scenario for the learner to undertake in relation to the assessment criteria

Advantages

👍 Supports identifying individuals who are struggling with a concept or subject

👍 Encourages independent thinking

👍 Can challenge a learner's potential

👍 Checks underpinning knowledge of the subject area

Disadvantages

👎 Can be time-consuming to plan, assess and to provide individual feedback

👎 Can cause some learners to feel anxious and overwhelmed

👎 Not accepted as summative assessment by all awarding organisations

> ### Tip
> Remember that some learners need time to process what they are doing before they can verbalise it. Be confident to allow silences and don't feel you need to speak or ask questions.

Further reading and weblinks

Gravells A (2016) *Principles and Practices of Assessment*: Learning Matters/SAGE, London.

Ollin R and Tucker J (2016) *The Vocational Assessor Handbook* (6th edn): Kogan Page, London.

47 Witness testimony

Individual	√	Small group		Large group	
Initial	*	Formative		Summative	√
Informal		Formal	√	Preparation and marking	√
Entry Level		Level 1 and 2	√	Level 3 upwards	√

*depends upon what and how you are planning to use the approach

What is it and where can it be used?

A witness testimony is a piece of evidence which states what a learner has achieved. It is assessed according to the required criteria, and included in the learner's portfolio. It should be completed by a subject expert who is familiar with the learner and their job role, usually the employer or supervisor in the workplace. The witness provides a written or recorded account of what the learner has done.

What can it be used for?

A witness testimony can be used as a formal supplementary piece of evidence which can be included in a portfolio as part of the summative assessment. It is a popular approach used mainly in work-based learning. For example, a learner studying the Level 2 Equine Groom Standards may ask their employer or supervisor to complete a witness testimony. This would be in regard to the routine yard and field duties they have carried out over a period of time.

Witness testimonies are particularly beneficial for work-based qualifications or standards which require the learner to perform jobs or tasks over a length of time in a range of conditions.

If you are asking the witness for a written testimony it is beneficial to provide them with a template to support them in forming a concise report. It's also useful for them to have a copy of the qualification specification or standards, so that they can ensure their testimony is relevant. They should sign and date the testimony to make it authentic. If they are making a recording (visual or aural), they should state their name, the date

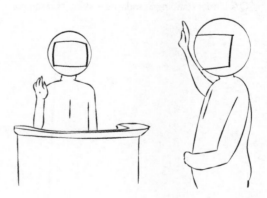

and time, and the person they are providing the testimony for, as well as the aspects their testimony covers.

Resources

- A subject expert to act as a witness for what the learner has achieved

Advantages

👍 Captures invaluable practical evidence which an assessor might not see, perhaps because it doesn't occur regularly

👍 Provides additional feedback to the learner regarding their progress and achievement

Disadvantages

👎 Can be time-consuming for the witness to write, and the assessor to read

👎 Can be difficult to authenticate

👎 The learner might write the testimony and ask the witness to sign it

👎 Witnesses might need guidance and support regarding how to write a concise testimony

---

Tip

Witness testimonies could be used to support video evidence of a learner undertaking a particular task or job role, where the assessor has not been able to.

Further reading and weblinks

Gravells A (2016) *Principles and Practices of Assessment*: Learning Matters/SAGE, London.

Petty G (2014) *Teaching Today*: Oxford University Press, Oxford.

SQA Understanding Standards – *Witness testimony* – https://tinyurl.com/y4no5e2t

48 Workplace documentation

Individual	√	Small group		Large group	
Initial		Formative	√	Summative	√
Informal	√	Formal	√	Preparation and marking	*
Entry Level	√	Level 1 and 2	√	Level 3 upwards	√

*depends upon what and how you are planning to use the approach

What is it and where can it be used?

Workplace documentation is about a learner providing examples of what they have used or completed as part of their training in the workplace. This can provide complementary or additional evidence for assessment.

Some jobs require staff to use or complete specific workplace documentation as part of their role. For example, a motor mechanic would use an automated job card detailing the work required to the vehicle. Or to start the production of an item in manufacturing, a job card is created from a work order. In catering and hospitality, accurate information must be given to customers including ingredients and prices.

What can it be used for?

With permission from the employer, learners can copy the workplace documentation, anonymise this, and include it in their portfolio of evidence (see Chapter 23) towards an assessment. For example, Level 2 Hospitality and Catering Principles require the learner to list the correct condiments, accompaniments and service equipment for different menu items. The learner could produce a written list and include a copy of the menu as additional evidence towards summative assessment. Or a learner studying a Level 3 Advanced Technical Extended Diploma in Land-based Engineering must complete records and vehicle handovers to customers, including recommendations on actions required. Copies of these records can be anonymised and included in the portfolio as additional evidence towards summative assessment.

When formally assessing workplace documentation, it's important to verify that it has been produced by the learner and that it meets the required outcomes.

Workplace documentation can also be used informally for training purposes and formative assessment, e.g. asking a learner to complete tasks from a job card within a simulated environment, and then providing constructive feed-back on how they can improve their performance for future assessment.

Resources

- Photocopier or a device to capture an image of the evidence

Advantages

- Encourages independent-thinking skills
- Develops employability skills
- Results can be seen immediately

Disadvantages

- Requires permission from the employer
- Can be difficult to prove the learner actually used a specific document without further evidence

---

Tip

As well as seeking permission from the employer to use the documents, if a learner is providing evidence which includes confidential or customer details, these should always be anonymised or covered up.

Further reading and weblinks

Petty G (2009) *Evidence-based Teaching: A Practical Approach* (2nd edn): Nelson Thornes, Cheltenham.

Training Qualifications UK – *The ins and outs of performance evidence* – https://tinyurl.com/yxmvjoz7

49 Worksheet

Individual	√	Small group	√	Large group	√
Initial	√	Formative	√	Summative	√
Informal	√	Formal	√	Preparation and marking	√
Entry Level	√	Level 1 and 2	√	Level 3 upwards	√

What is it and where can it be used?

A worksheet is an interactive document (either paper based or digital), which learners read and respond to. You can develop your own worksheets to suit your subject, levels, assessment requirements, and the various learning styles of your learners. Often you can download these free from the internet (just search for your topic or subject).

The worksheet could be question based, e.g. a list of ten open questions, or multi-choice questions where the learner has to select the correct answer. These could be designed for the learner to fill in blank spaces in sentences (also known as a gapped handout), e.g. paragraphs of text with key words missing for the learner to work out and fill in.

Worksheets can be used during your session formally under examination conditions, or they can be used informally as an individual, paired or small group assessment activity. They can also be set as a homework task, but the authenticity of the work would need to be confirmed with the learner.

What can it be used for?

A worksheet can be used informally to formatively assess a learner's progress or starting point. Alternatively, it could be used formally as a summative assessment approach to provide evidence of a learner's knowledge.

A worksheet can also be used like a handout. It could provide information about a topic for the learner to read, followed by questions for them to answer. Completed examples could be given to learners for them to peer assess each other's responses (see Chapter 21).

Learners might be undertaking a vocational qualification which requires them to demonstrate their knowledge and skills in the subject, but not necessarily to have high English reading and writing skills. One of the key benefits of using a worksheet as a formative assessment approach is the ability to differentiate between learners. For example, you may have some learners identifying technical words in a word search, whereas others are completing a crossword by answering questions about the same words. Alternatively, you may have some learners writing down their answers to questions, whereas others are circling multi-choice answers. All learners are demonstrating their knowledge by completing the differentiated worksheets.

Resources

- A relevant worksheet
- Pens and paper or a suitable electronic device

Advantages

👍 Can be used to differentiate learning and assessment

👍 Particularly useful for lower-level learners

👍 Can be used as a group or individual approach

Disadvantages

👎 Time-consuming to produce (but can be used for future learners)

👎 If set as a homework task it can be difficult to authenticate

👎 Mature learners might consider them inappropriate

> **Tip**
>
> If you are producing your own worksheets, ask a colleague to proofread your text prior to sharing this with the learners, to ensure there are no spelling or typing errors.

Further reading and weblinks

Gravells A (2016) *Principles and Practices of Assessment*: Learning Matters/SAGE, London.

Mansell S (2019) *50 Teaching and Learning Approaches*: Learning Matters/SAGE, London.

Petty G (2014) *Teaching Today*: Oxford University Press, Oxford.

50 Written tests and examinations

Individual	√	Small group	√	Large group	√
Initial	√	Formative	√	Summative	√
Informal	√	Formal	√	Preparation and marking	√
Entry Level	√	Level 1 and 2	√	Level 3 upwards	√

What is it and where can it be used?

A written test or an examination is an assessment approach intended to measure a learner's competence, skills, behaviours, attitudes, knowledge and/or understanding. A test is usually less formal and taken in a shorter time than an examination. If the written test or examination is being used informally it can usually be taken anywhere appropriate, and is often referred to as a mock test or mock exam. If it is being used formally, an official area must be set up and invigilators used to oversee the process. This is to ensure learners are not communicating with anyone, and it is fair for all. Most written tests and examinations have a limited amount of time for the learners to complete within, however not all learners will complete in the time. Some awarding organisations stipulate the date a formal test or examination must be taken, with a start and end time.

Written tests and examinations are often used as part of the end-point assessment for a range of apprenticeship standards. This is in place of historical continual assessment. When a learner is ready to take the end-point assessment, their employer or training provider will put them forward for the assessment via an independent end-point assessment organisation who has no affiliation with the learner, employer or learning provider.

Written tests and examinations are sometimes undertaken online. They might be set and marked online, or the assessor could create them using relevant software and also mark them.

What can it be used for?

Written tests and examinations are a great way to assess the progress your learners are making towards their targets. They enable you to measure competence, skills, behaviours, attitudes, knowledge and/or understanding, and can be used throughout a programme of study formally or informally. For example, a learner who is going to be taking a formal maths written test or examination could practise by undertaking mock tests or mock exams.

Recognised accredited formal written tests and examinations, e.g. a General Certificate of Secondary Education (GCSE) or an Apprenticeship Standard, are often valued by employers and can really enhance a learner's curriculum vitae (CV) or job application.

Resources

- The written test or examination
- Pens and paper or access to an electronic device if online
- An area which can be adjusted to meet any examination conditions

Advantages

- Determines the effectiveness of your teaching
- A large number of learners can be tested at the same time
- A handy way to regularly check progress

Disadvantages

- Only judges a learner's ability in set conditions on that day
- Learners may get anxious and may not perform to their best ability
- Learners might misunderstand the questions
- Does not teach long-term thinking skills
- Could be a risk of just teaching and preparing for the written test or examination and not developing wider skills
- Can be high pressure on the organisation to achieve good learner results
- Secure storage of documents is required before and afterwards, if this is breached, cheating could take place

> ## Tip
>
> When using mock tests or mock exams, set the area up as if it were the real thing. This will allow learners to experience and understand exam conditions and what to expect on the day.

Further reading and weblinks

Institute for Apprenticeships and Technical Education – *Developing an end-point assessment plan* – https://tinyurl.com/y4pam4h7

Joint Council for Qualifications (JCQ) – *Instructions for conducting GCSE and GCE* – https://tinyurl.com/y4lma8h7

Appendix 1

Apprenticeship programmes

Assessing apprenticeship programmes

If you are training an apprentice during their programme, you must prepare them for end-point assessment (EPA). You will need to see the *apprenticeship assessment plan* to find out what's involved, e.g. ensuring the apprentice knows how to take part in a professional discussion or how to give a presentation.

Assessment is therefore formative, and many of the approaches in this book will be useful to help you check progress. Summative assessment will be by the end-point assessor, who will never have met the apprentice prior to the EPA.

If the apprentice is also working towards a qualification as part of their programme, it's probable that you will be able to assess both formatively and summatively. This is providing you meet the requirements of the qualification's assessment strategy.

Apprenticeship assessment plans

In England, the term assessment plan for an apprenticeship programme is not the same as an assessment plan for a learner working towards a qualification. An apprenticeship assessment plan outlines the way in which the full programme will be assessed for a particular occupation. It might or might not include a relevant qualification. If it does, the normal qualification requirements of formative and summative assessment will apply.

Whilst the nature and methods of assessment will differ between occupations and job roles, all assessment plans will focus on the end-point (synoptic) assessment process and will:

* explain in detail what will be assessed (i.e. knowledge, skills and behaviours)
* explain how the apprentice will be assessed (i.e. which method or methods will be used to judge competency at the end of the apprenticeship programme)
* indicate who will carry out the assessment (i.e. who will be the assessor(s) for each aspect of the end-point assessment) and who will make the final decision regarding the competency and grading descriptors: grades of distinction, merit, pass and not yet achieved (NYA) will be used
* propose quality assurance arrangements to make sure that the assessment is reliable and consistent across different locations, employers, training and assessment organisations

Apprenticeship standards

Each occupation to be assessed will have an *apprenticeship standard* which outlines details of:

- the occupation/job profile
- the knowledge, skills and behaviours required to perform the job role
- the entry requirements
- the level of the programme and the typical time allowed to achieve it
- whether any qualifications are also included which must be achieved prior to the apprentice taking the end-point assessment, along with any other subjects such as English and maths
- links to relevant professional association registration and progression (if applicable)
- when the standard will be reviewed

The standard will be used by the person training the apprentice to ensure all aspects are met. However, the standard should not be treated like a list which is ticked off when the apprentice has achieved something. This is often referred to as the *tick box culture*, i.e. ticking things off and then moving on to something else. Whilst the apprentice might feel they have achieved something, they may not be able to competently do it again in a month's time. The apprentice will need to demonstrate their competence over time, not just on one occasion, hence the use of end-point assessment.

Further reading and weblinks

Apprenticeship standards and plans – www.gov.uk/guidance/search-for-apprenticeship-standards

Armitage A and Cogger A (2019) *The New Apprenticeships: Facilitating Learning, Mentoring, Coaching and Assessing:* Critical Publishing, Northwich/St Albans – https://amzn.to/33MsAdw

Read H (2016) *The Best Assessor's Guide: Essential Knowledge and Skills for Vocational Assessors* (Apprenticeship edition): Read On Publications Ltd, Bideford – https://amzn.to/2Bu5wEr

Appendix 2
Marking and grading

The difference between marking and grading

There is a difference between marking and grading. A simplistic way of remembering this is that a mark is given for the achievement of certain aspects from a programme of learning, whereas a grade is given for the overall achievement of the full programme. If you are assessing towards a qualification or an apprenticeship programme, guidance on how to do this should be available. However, if you are devising your own assessment activities, you will need to decide on what basis you will mark and/or grade. It's also useful to have an exemplar answer for any questions you will use. This will give you a benchmark to compare the learners' answers to, and to allocate your marks, e.g. by giving a mark out of 10, or a percentage for an essay. Feedback should also be given to help the learner develop and to improve their English.

Grading is about establishing the overall level of achievement for a full programme of learning, e.g. by assigning an A, B or C, based on the results (or marks) of all the aspects a learner has achieved.

It will very much depend upon the programme you are assessing, as to whether you will mark and/or grade, or if you will just make a decision as to whether your learner has passed or not. However, all marking and grading should be based on what is being assessed, i.e. the assessment criteria, rather than on personal opinions.

Some qualifications might be achieved by a pass or a fail, e.g. a multiple-choice test where learners must achieve seven out of ten for a pass. However, learners with excellent subject knowledge or occupational competence can often fail tests because they don't understand the test process. Online multiple-choice tests are a very effective, instant and low-cost way to test learners. However, because learners can perceive these as quick and easy, they might have a tendency not to read the questions properly, or just guess the answers.

Analysing learner achievement

At some point, you might need to analyse your learners' achievements, perhaps for statistical and auditing purposes. This could be by comparing your learners' results to benchmark figures or targets, or by comparing their achievements to each other's or to different cohorts.

If there is more than one person assessing the same subject at your organisation, you should standardise your practice with them. This would include sharing and comparing assessment activities, expected responses, and the decisions made.

Norm referencing

If you want to compare the achievements of a group of learners against one another, you could use *norm referencing* which is a form of grading in addition to marking.

Norm referencing will proportion your grades accordingly, as there will always be those in your group who will achieve a high grade, and those who will achieve a low grade, leaving the rest in the middle. You would therefore allocate grades according to a quota, e.g. the top 20 per cent would achieve an A, the next 20 per cent a B, and so on. Norm referencing uses the achievement of a group to set the standards for specific grades, or for how many learners will pass or fail. This type of assessment is useful to maintain consistency of results over time; whether the test questions are easy or hard, there will always be those achieving a high grade and those achieving a lower grade.

Example

Joan has a group of 25 learners who have just taken a test consisting of 20 questions and she wants to allocate grades A–E to her group. She has worked out the top 20 per cent will achieve an A, the second 20 per cent a B and so on. When she marks the tests, she is surprised to see the lowest mark was 16 out of 20, meaning a grade E. Even though the learners had done well in the test, they were still given a low grade in comparison to the rest of the group.

A fairer method would have been to just set a pass mark, e.g. 15 out of 20, and not use grading at all. Learners achieving 14 or below could be referred and retake a different test at a later date.

Criterion referencing

Criterion referencing enables learners to achieve based upon their own merit, as their achievements are not compared with one another. All learners therefore have equality of opportunity. If grades are allocated, e.g. a distinction, credit, pass or refer, there will be specific criteria which must have been met for each. These criteria are usually supplied by the awarding organisation if learners are taking an accredited qualification.

Example

Refer – did not describe the activity

Pass – described the activity

Credit – described and analysed the activity

Distinction – described, analysed and critically reflected upon the activity

If learners are eligible to retake a test, it's advisable to leave a period of time, e.g. seven days, before they take it again. If learners are taking a test which other learners have already attempted, you will need to ensure they have not communicated their responses. If learners feel the urge to cheat, they are ultimately only cheating themselves. A bank of questions would be useful; this way you could choose a certain number of random questions that will always be different when put together in a test. Computer-generated question papers will automatically choose different questions for different learners and tests.

Results analysis

If you assess a programme which requires grades to be given to learners in addition to marking, you will need to analyse the results regarding their achievements. The grades for analysis could be expressed as:

- 1, 2, 3, 4, 5
- A, B, C, D, E
- achieved/not achieved
- competent/not yet competent
- distinction, credit, pass, fail
- pass, refer, fail
- percentages, e.g. 80 per cent
- satisfactory, good, outstanding

Analysing the results will help you see not only how well your learners have done, but also whether or not there are any trends. For example, if all your learners received an average of C, but another assessor's group achieved an average of B, is there a fault on your part?

If you had a group of 30 learners who all achieved an A grade, was this due to your excellent support, the skills and knowledge of your learners, or by your being too lenient when assessing? Having sample answers to compare your learners' responses to will help you remain objective.

If you had a group of 15 learners who all failed an assignment, you could ask yourself the same questions. However, it could be that the assignment questions were worded in a confusing way, or you had given the assignment too early in the programme. If most of your group averaged a grade of 50 per cent, whereas a colleague's group averaged 80 per cent, was this because you had given your learners misleading or ambiguous information relating to that topic?

Asking yourself these questions will help you ascertain if you are producing assessments that are fit for purpose, and if not, you will need to do something about it, e.g. you may need to amend your teaching or assessment methods, reword your questions, or redesign some assessment activities.

Further reading and weblinks

Gravells A (2016) *Principles and Practices of Assessment*: Learning Matters/SAGE, London.

Appendix 3
Making assessment decisions and providing feedback to learners

Making a decision

Once assessment has taken place, you will need to make a decision as to your learners' progress and achievements, and then provide feedback.

You must always remain *objective*, i.e. by making a decision based on learners' competence towards set criteria. You should not be *subjective*, i.e. by making a decision based on your own opinions or other factors such as a learner's personality. When making a decision, you will need to base it on everything you have assessed. If you are observing a learner's skills, you could follow this up by asking questions to check their knowledge and understanding.

You may find, when assessing, that your learners haven't achieved everything they should have. You need to base your decision on all the information and evidence available to you at the time. If a learner has not met all the requirements, you need to give constructive feedback, discuss any inconsistencies or gaps, and give advice on what they should do next. If a learner disagrees with the assessment process or your decision, they are entitled to follow your organisation's appeals procedure. Don't get too engrossed with your administrative work or form filling when making a decision, that you forget to inform the learner what they have achieved.

Your decisions should always be valid, authentic, reliable, current and sufficient (VARCS). You should also be fair and ethical when assessing learners, making a decision and providing feedback.

- Fair: the assessment activity was appropriate to all learners at the required level, was inclusive (i.e. available to all), and differentiated for any particular needs. All learners had an equal chance of an accurate assessment decision.
- Ethical: the methods used were right and proper for what was assessed and the context of the assessment. The learner's welfare, health, safety and security were not compromised.

Providing feedback

Feedback can be given informally, e.g. during a discussion, or formally, after an assessment activity. It can be verbal or written depending upon the type of assessment you have carried out. If you are with learners, e.g. observing an activity, you can give verbal feedback immediately (do keep written records of all formal assessments). If you are assessing work which has been handed in for marking, you can give written feedback later. Written can also mean by electronic means.

The term *feed-forward* relates to the next steps of the learner journey, i.e. going forward, as opposed to going back over what they have done. It is about the future development of a learner, which could relate to the next unit, qualification, or on-the-job activity.

It's always useful to start by asking a learner how they think they have done. This gives them the opportunity to identify their own mistakes before you have to tell them. Comments which specifically focus on the activity or work produced, rather than the individual, will be more helpful and motivating to learners.

The advantages of providing feedback are that it:

- can boost your learner's confidence and motivation
- creates opportunities for clarification, discussion and progression
- emphasises progress rather than failure
- enables learners to appreciate what they need to do to improve or change their practice
- identifies further learning opportunities or actions required
- informs learners of what they have achieved

You should always provide feedback in a way which will make it clear how your learner has met the requirements, what they have achieved (or not), and what they need to do next.

When providing feedback, you should always try to be:

- constructive – to help retain a learner's motivation
- specific – by being factual and stating exactly what was achieved or not achieved
- developmental – by encouraging further learning, e.g. reading and research

You need to make sure you are not being ambiguous or vague, i.e. leaving a learner not knowing what they have achieved or what they have to do next. You need to be factual regarding what they have achieved in relation to the assessment criteria, and not just give your opinion. It is important to keep learners motivated, and what you say can help or hinder their progress and confidence.

Often, the focus of feedback is likely to be on mistakes rather than strengths. If something positive is stated first, any negative comments are more likely to be listened to and acted upon. Starting with a negative point may discourage your learner from listening to anything else that is said. If possible, start with something positive, then state what could be improved, and finish on a developmental note. This sandwiches the negative aspect between two positive or helpful aspects. However, negative feedback if given skilfully can help a learner if used in the right way. You will need to find out if your organisation has any specific feedback methods they wish you to use, which will ensure a standardised approach across all assessors to all learners. Whatever method you use to give feedback, it should always be backed up by a written record.

Different feedback methods

There are many ways you can give feedback to learners. These include being:

- descriptive – describe examples of what was achieved, what could be improved and why. Using this method lets you describe what a learner has done, how they met the required assessment criteria, and what they can do to progress further.

- evaluative – usually just a grade such as eight out of ten, or a statement such as *well done* or *good*. This method is not descriptive and does not offer helpful or constructive advice. It does not give learners the opportunity to know what was well done, what was good about it, or how they could improve. It's just an evaluation of achievement which doesn't offer detailed feedback.

- constructive – is specific and focused to confirm a learner's achievement or to give developmental points in a positive and helpful way.

- destructive – relates to improvements which are needed and is often given in a negative way which could demoralise the learner.

- objective – clearly relates to specific assessment requirements and is factual regarding what has and has not been met.

- subjective – is often just a personal opinion which can be biased, e.g. if the assessor is friendly with the learner. Feedback might be vague and not based on the assessment requirements.

When giving feedback to learners you need to be aware that it could affect their self-esteem and whether they continue with the programme or not. The quality of feedback received can be a key factor towards their progress, and the ability to learn new knowledge and skills. Ongoing constructive feedback which is developmental and has been carefully thought through is an indication of your interest in the learner, and your intention to help them develop and do well in the future.

When providing feedback:

- own your statements by beginning with the word "*I*" rather than "*you*" (however, written feedback could be given in the third person if your organisation prefers)

- start with something positive, e.g. "*I really liked the confident manner in which you delivered your presentation*"

- be specific about what you have seen, e.g. "*I felt the way you explained that topic was really interesting due to your knowledge and humour*" or "*I found the way you explained that topic was rather confusing to me*"

- offer constructive and specific follow-on points, e.g. "*I feel I would have understood it better if you had broken the subject down into smaller stages*"

- end with something positive or developmental, e.g. "*I enjoyed your presentation – you had prepared well and came across as very organised and professional*", or "*I enjoyed your session, however, issuing a handout summarising the key points would be really helpful to refer to after the session*"

Being constructive, specific and developmental with what you say, and owning your statements by beginning with the word "*I*", should help a learner focus on what you are saying and listen to how they can improve. If you don't have any follow-on points then don't create them just for the sake of it. Conversely, if you do have any negative points or criticisms, don't say "*My only negative point is …*" or "*My only criticisms are …*". It's much better to replace these words and say "*Some areas for development could be …*" instead.

Further reading and weblinks

Gravells A (2016) *Principles and Practices of Assessment*: Learning Matters/SAGE, London.

Appendix 4

Quality assurance

What is quality assurance?

Quality assurance is about having systems in place to ensure that the assessment process is valid and reliable and has been undertaken with integrity.

If quality assurance does not take place, there could be risks to the accuracy, consistency and fairness of training and assessment practice. Quality assurance should be a continual process with the aim of maintaining and improving the products and services offered.

If there is no external formal examination taken by learners, there has to be a system of monitoring the performance of trainers and assessors and the experiences of the learners. If not, assessors might make incorrect judgements or pass a learner who hasn't met the requirements, perhaps because they were biased towards them or had made a mistake. If you are assessing an accredited qualification or a programme of learning, there will be an internal quality assurer who will monitor your practice and check your decisions.

Internal quality assurance

Internal quality assurance (IQA) relates to the monitoring of all the teaching, learning and assessment activities which learners, trainees or employees will undertake. Internal quality assurance is not something that is added on to the end of a qualification or a programme of learning. It should be carried out on an ongoing basis with a view to making improvements, or keeping the status quo if everything is satisfactory. Records must be maintained of all monitoring activities to prove they actually took place and to facilitate improvements as necessary.

There are other terms used for internal quality assurance which you might come across. e.g. internal *verification* and internal *moderation*.

Often, internal quality assurers are also experienced trainers and assessors in the subject area they are quality assuring, e.g. if the subject area is motor vehicle maintenance, they should not be internally quality assuring other subjects they are not experienced in, such as horticulture. The IQA process might be the same for each subject, but the internal quality assurer must be fully familiar with what is being assessed to make a valid and reliable decision. Valid means you are doing what you should, and reliable means you would get similar results each time you did it.

As an internal quality assurer only *samples* various activities, there is the possibility that some aspects might be missed. Imagine this taking place in a bakery – the quality assurer would not sample every item by tasting each one made, they would only taste a sample from each baker, otherwise there would be nothing left to sell. This means there are often risks involved with sampling.

External quality assurance

External quality assurance (EQA) relates to the monitoring of training, assessment and IQA processes within a centre which has been approved by an awarding organisation (AO) to deliver and assess their qualifications. Any organisation can become an approved centre providing they meet the qualification and the AO's requirements.

External quality assurance must take place on behalf of an awarding organisation to ensure the learners who have been registered with them have received a quality service. It also seeks to ensure that training, assessment and internal quality assurance have been conducted in a consistent, safe and fair manner.

Your learners, when they successfully complete a qualification, will receive a certificate with the awarding organisation's name on as well as the centre's name. Therefore the EQA must ensure everything is in order, or their reputation, as well as the centre's, could be brought into disrepute.

Further reading and weblinks

Gravells A (2016) *Principles and Practices of Quality Assurance*: Learning Matters/SAGE, London.

Read H (2012) *The Best Quality Assurer's Guide*: Read On Publications, Bedeford/St Albans – https://amzn.to/2MYAKsD

Index